Printing Teacher's Guide

for *My Printing Book*

Grade 1

and *Printing Power*

Grade 2

by Jan Z. Olsen, OTR

Developer of the Handwriting Without Tears® curriculum

Handwriting Without Tears®
Jan Z. Olsen, OTR

8001 MacArthur Blvd
Cabin John, MD 20818
Phone: 301–263–2700 • Fax: 301–263–2707
www.hwtears.com • JanOlsen@hwtears.com

Printing Teacher's Guide

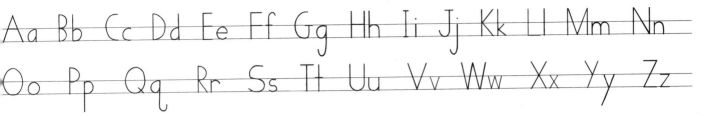

Aa Bb Cc Dd Ee Ff Gg Hh Ii Jj Kk Ll Mm Nn
Oo Pp Qq Rr Ss Tt Uu Vv Ww Xx Yy Zz

Welcome to the Handwriting Without Tears® method! I'm Jan Olsen, the developer of the program. I'm an occupational therapist and have specialized in handwriting for more than 25 years.

Handwriting Without Tears® is a simple, developmentally based curriculum for writing readiness, printing, and cursive. The multisensory lessons teach to all learning styles—visual, auditory, tactile, and kinesthetic. The unique materials and appealing workbooks eliminate problems with letter formation, reversals, legibility, sentence spacing, and cursive connections. Teachers, parents, and children find the program enjoyable, even fun, and the results very satisfying.

It is my goal to make handwriting available to all children as an automatic and natural skill. Children who write well perform better in school, enjoy their classes more, and feel proud of their work.

Introduction

Printing Teacher's Guide is the guide to the student workbooks, *My Printing Book* (Grade 1) and *Printing Power* (Grade 2). The tips and lesson plans in this guide will help you be a great handwriting teacher.

You will learn how the HWT letter style, teaching order, workbook design, and unique teaching strategies make printing easier for children. There are suggestions for fun ways to help children with posture, pencil grip, and paper placement. The simple lesson plans make teaching a breeze.

Keep the lessons short and fun—you will appreciate how well your children write.

Jan Z. Olsen

Table of Contents

Take a Look at *My Printing Book* (Grade 1)

My Printing Book is for first graders or children at that level. *My Printing Book* has a bright yellow cover but you won't find Grade 1 on it. That's out of consideration for older children who are working at a Grade 1 level.

Capital letters are reviewed at the beginning of the book. They are the foundation for lowercase printing. The emphasis of *My Printing Book* is on printing lowercase letters correctly and using them in words and sentences. Complete number lessons are at the back of the book and these pages should be taught along with your math instruction.

The left-hand pages have huge step-by-step instructions for each new letter. The teacher demonstrates each step and checks to be sure the children will practice the letter correctly.

The right-hand pages have word practice. The new letter is used with previously taught letters. This provides a nice balance of new and review work.

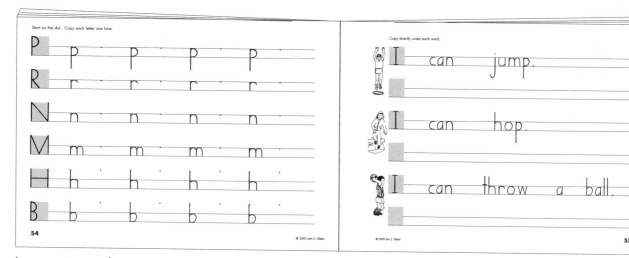

Letter review and sentence practice pages are presented after each letter group.

Printing Power is for second graders or older beginners. *Printing Power* has a bright turquoise cover but you won't find Grade 2 on it. That's out of consideration for older children who are working at a Grade 2 level.

Capital letters and numbers are reviewed at the beginning of the book. *Printing Power* uses one page for each letter, with step-by-step instructions and simple word practice. *Printing Power* uses smaller size printing for sentences, paragraph, and word game pages. Complete number lessons are at the back of the book and should be taught along with your math instruction.

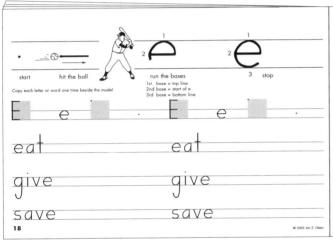

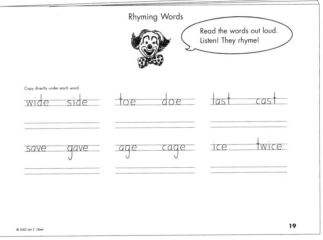

Wide double lines are used for letter instruction and simple word practice.

A smaller size is used for language arts word activities, sentences, and paragraphs.

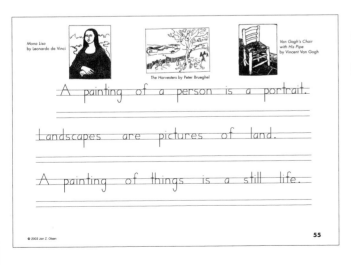

Printing Power helps children develop speed and neatness with a variety of interesting sentence and paragraph pages.

Tips for You

The tips and lesson plans in this guide will help you be a great handwriting teacher. If you are like most educators, parents or therapists, you've had minimal or no handwriting training. Based on responses from tens of thousands of teacher at our workshops, we know that only ten percent of elementary teachers have received any previous training. Without training, many teachers just pass out workbooks and neglect teaching. We don't want you to do that! Combined with your personal teaching style, our program will enable you to bring the program alive for your students with active and dynamic instruction. Parents, administrators, you, and most importantly the children will be delighted with your students' great success.

Teach a Short, Daily Handwriting Lesson

Just make a little time for handwriting, the payoff is so great. There are pressures from everywhere to cram more stuff into the instructor's day and it is very difficult. Making time for handwriting, however, will make it easier for you to fit everything else in! Spending a little time everyday with Handwriting Without Tears®, you will no longer have painfully slow writers, sloppy writers, kids avoiding writing altogether and there will be no more time wasted struggling to read your student's work.

Three Stages of Learning

Children learn to write correctly and easily when instructions follow these three developmentally based stages.

Stage 1—Imitation
The teacher demonstrates how to write the word cat. The child imitates the teacher to write cat. Think of this analogy—It is easiest to draw a horse when you have someone to show you step-by-step how to do it. You imitate.

Stage 2—Copying
There is a model of the word cat on a practice page. The child copies cat by looking at the image. Think of this analogy—It is easy to draw a horse when you have a picture of a horse to look at. You copy.

Stage 3—Independent Writing
There is no demonstration and there is no model of the word cat. The child writes cat on their own. Think of this analogy—It is a challenge to draw a horse when you have to do it from memory. You draw it independently.

Teaching at stage one, with lots of active demonstration makes it so much easier for children to learn. Your dynamic demonstrations will teach to their visual, auditory and kinesthetic learning styles. Once children can imitate correctly, they are ready to copy from the models in the workbooks. Children who can copy well are ready for independent writing. Anytime a child is struggling take them back to an easier stage.

Work on good habits

English is a top to bottom, left to right language. That's the way we read and write! The top to bottom habit is the key to printing quickly and neatly. Children who start letters at the top don't have to think about making letters. They print automatically and are able to print quickly without becoming sloppy. Starting at the bottom causes difficulty because it is impossible to write with speed without becoming sloppy. This demonstration proves the importance of starting at the top. Try it!

Make 5 lines down.   Make 5 lines, alternating down/up.   Now do it again, very fast.

By starting at the top, you can be both fast and neat. Children who start letters at the bottom are either slow or sloppy. In this guide, you'll learn how to correct bad habits and emphasize good habits with easy and fun techniques.

Grade 1 Teachers

ese tips will help you customize how you use *My Printing Book* to meet your teaching
jectives and the needs of your children.

aching first grade is wonderful. You have:
- Very young children whose outlook and habits can be shaped.
- Eager, hopeful children who are excited to be learning to write.

aching first grade is a challenge too. You face:
- Children with significant differences in age and developmental abilities.
- Children with very different preschool and kindergarten preparation.

ips for Lessons

ompliment your reading curriculum
ecause reading and handwriting are different skills, the letter order for reading instruction will not always match the order
ed for handwriting.

his is the way it should be. Reading and phonics programs teach (or should teach) in a letter order that is easiest for the
hildren developmentally. Handwriting programs should as well. When there is overlap, do activities that explore and
ghlight the link. When there is not overlap just teach the skills independently until it is appropriate to combine them. "Now
e are learning to write the letter b, do you remember what sound the letter b makes?"

your reading or phonics curriculum doesn't lend itself to this type of teaching, you can introduce some letters out of order
follow the tip below for quickly previewing all letters. Please remember, however, that the order in which we introduce
e letters for writing is the easiest order for children to learn to write.

ay good-bye to bad habits
re they starting letters at the bottom, or making reversals? Don't despair. HWT has a secret strategy to prevent children
om using those bad habits. See the fun, mystery games on pages 3 and 20 of the *My Printing Book* workbook. Read about
is strategy on pages 18 and 40 of this guide.

review all lowercase letters
 preview all the lowercase letters quickly, go through the whole workbook using just the letter formation pages and one or
o words on the facing page. Then go back and work through the whole book page by page.

each names
or right now, let children who don't know lowercase letters use all capitals for their name. But, individually teach these
hildren the needed lowercase letters so they can write their name in the capital and lowercase form.

ips for Teaching Children of All Ability Levels

eep skilled printers occupied
ll the children who finish quickly to color the picture. The black and white illustrations and extra space are designed
specially for coloring and drawing.

Meet the needs of all children
ou can be teaching the same letter to all your children. Some may need to learn that letter with a wood piece lesson,
hers with the "wet–dry–try" slate activity, and others are ready for the workbook page. You can accommodate individual
arning styles and different ability levels.

elp children who don't speak English
he large step-by-step illustrations for letter formation do not require reading ability to follow. Easy words, picture cues, and
peated sentence patterns (C is for cow. O is for owl.) make the book friendly for children just learning English.

Grade 1 Teachers continued . . .

Tips for Grades, Homework and Parents

Send home letter formation chart

Copy the page with capital, number, and lowercase letter formation chart from the back of this Teacher's Guide. Send it home with a note similar to this:

Dear Parents:

We are using the Handwriting Without Tears® curriculum. This chart shows you how to make the letters and numbers. We will be learning the capital letters first. See **www.hwtears.com** for more information about this curriculum. We are excited about helping your child develop good handwriting skills.

Be fair about grading

The purpose of grades is to communicate, to let children and parents know how they're doing. All children who try should be able to earn a very good grade in handwriting. Children will usually try hard and make excellent progress with supportive instruction and short assignments.

Avoid handwriting homework

Your students' work in class and with *My Printing Book* is generally sufficient. If a child needs extra support, give parents suggestions for helping. Such help should take just five minutes per day.

Respect other styles

Your children may have used a different curriculum. Always accept different styles. Allow children to use another style even if the letters do not match what is in the workbook. Do insist that letters be formed and placed correctly.

Grade 2 Teachers

These tips will help you customize how you use *Printing Power* to meet your teaching objectives and the needs of your children.

Teaching second grade is delightful. You have:
- Children who are older, more capable, and responsible.
- Children who have mastered many basic reading and writing school skills.

Teaching second grade is a challenge too. You face:
- Children who are getting behind and discouraged about writing.
- Children with bad habits for writing.

Tips for Lessons

Review all lowercase letters
If you would like to quickly review all of the lowercase letters, just go through the workbook using only the letter formation pages. Then return to the beginning and work through the whole book page by page.

Pace your lessons
Let your children guide you. Start out slowly. Do not think they have to finish a page a day. Some pages take longer. Be relaxed and pick a pace that is very comfortable for 80 percent of your children. Accommodate the other children with somewhat different lessons.

Tips for Teaching All Children

Meet the needs of all children
Accommodate slower children by assigning less work. For instance, you can have them do the letter instruction and word pages and skip the sentence and word game pages. This way the slower children can keep up with the class for letter lessons. Also, give extra support by using lots of demonstration and imitation, and multi-sensory instruction. For advanced students, supplement the workbook lessons with creative writing and other language arts activities.

Help children who don't speak English
The illustrated step-by-step letter demonstrations require no reading ability for the child to learn how to form the letters. Although children may not be able to fully understand the content, they will be able to copy the words and sentences.

Tips for Grades, Homework, and Parents

Send home letter formation chart
Copy the page with capital, number, and lowercase letter formation chart from the back of this Teacher's Guide. Send it home with a note similar to this:

> Dear Parents:
>
> We are using the Handwriting Without Tears® curriculum. This chart shows you how to make the letters and numbers. We will be learning the capital letters first. See **www.hwtears.com** for more information about this curriculum. We are excited about helping your child develop good handwriting skills.

Be fair about grading
The purpose of grades is to communicate, to let children and parents know how they're doing. All children who try should be able to earn a very good grade in handwriting. Children will usually try hard and make excellent progress with supportive instruction and short assignments.

Avoid handwriting homework
Your students' work in class and with *Printing Power* is generally sufficient. If a child needs extra support, give parents suggestions for helping. Such help should take just five minutes per day.

Parents and Homeschoolers

Teaching your own child is delightful. You have:
- More freedom to adjust the pace to your child's needs and abilities.
- More ability to provide individual attention.

Teaching your own child is a challenge too. You may have:
- A child who has had negative school experiences with handwriting.
- Insecurities about your ability to be an effective instructor.
- Difficulty balancing the roles of teacher and parent.

Tips for Lessons

Assure interest and cooperation
Don't go too fast. Parents are often so eager and pleased that they try to get their children to do just one more word or one more sentence. Resist the temptation. Keep lessons short (10 to 15 minutes) and have your child practice for only about 5 minutes of that time.

Balance reading and handwriting
Your child might have very different reading and handwriting skills. Remember that while both are language skills, handwriting requires fine motor and perceptual skills. When the child's language arts skills are much more advanced than handwriting skills, use other ways (dictation and keyboarding) to get around written work while the handwriting skills catch up.

Teach informally as you go about life
Stuck in a grocery line? Look for letters! Many of the frustrations of everyday life can be turned into pleasant, worthwhile experiences if you look for something around you to share with your child. Books are wonderful, but signs will do when you're out and about.

Select the appropriate materials for your child
There are no grade levels on the outside of our workbooks. Pick the right book for your child regardless of your child's age or grade level. Check our Web site, **www.hwtears.com**, for helpful tips about determining which book is right for your child

Tips for Working Together

Consult with your child's teacher
Your child and your child's teacher need to be comfortable with what you're doing. Sometimes teachers are very loyal to a particular method or system. Try to understand this, but communicate that your primary loyalty is to your child and what works for your child. Most teachers will support parents who approach them with respect and a desire to help.

Therapists and Specialists

Assisting children with handwriting problems is very satisfying. You have:
- Professional skills and experience that will help you serve the children.
- More ability to provide individual attention.

Assisting children with handwriting problems is a challenge too. You face:
- Children who are not able to keep up with their peers in handwriting.
- Limited time for consultations.

Tips for Working with Others

Look at more than the child
Ask the parent, teacher, and child what seems to be the problem. Then look at the child's papers from school and a copy of the workbook the child has been using. Watch the child write. Assess the child's physical habits for writing (posture, pencil grip, helping hand, paper placement) and the child's writing skills, memory, and letter and word formation habits. Finally, try to observe the child in the classroom or talk to the child's teacher. As a consultant, you'll assess the child but also try to assess the child's learning environment. These observations will help you pinpoint where you need to focus your efforts.

Good handwriting helps children with all school subjects.

Evaluate the curriculum
Examine the curriculum the child is using and then consider what you have identified as the problem. For example, if a child is running words together, and the current papers don't give enough room to write, say that. Always approach this issue in terms of what will work best for the child. Be specific and communicate to teachers and parents in a problem-solving way.

Achieve continuity when you see students infrequently
Cooperate with the people at school. Talk to parents and volunteers. Help them and show them what you're doing so they will help your students. Some therapists give children more time by working in groups.

Tips for Lessons

Avoid dot to dot letter tracing and other inappropriate tasks
Often children with special needs are given work that is totally inappropriate. A perfect example is the common practice of dot to dot name tracing. Children may trace dots for years and not be able to write their names. Here's why. They're just trying to get from one dot to the next dot. They don't "see" each letter as a whole. For the best results, use developmentally appropriate materials and strategies.

Manage unrealistic expectations
The primary mistake many instructors make is expecting too much writing. Just requiring less writing does wonders. But the work itself may be too hard. If the child hates writing, has stopped trying, or doesn't improve, the work is too hard. Make it easier by using more demonstration and imitation, multisensory strategies, and easier papers.

Preparing for Paper and Pencil

1. **READY** Your Room—Simple room preparations will enhance your effectiveness.

2. **SET** Your Children Up—Fun strategies will promote good posture, paper placement, and pencil grip.

3. **GO** for It! Let the teaching begin.

Prepare Your Room

Places everybody! — Classroom style
Sometimes the most obvious things are overlooked. Children need to face the board when you demonstrate. That means standard classroom style. It's not just a matter of vision either. If they are facing you, they'll hear more clearly. That's because ears are shaped to catch sound. When children face you, their ears are in the best position to hear you. This is so simple and so amazing. Even if you need to have the children move the desks, do it! They will see, hear, and pay attention better.

Keep board space clear
You need lots of room to demonstrate letters, words, and sentences. Resist any temptation to use the board as a bulletin board.

Display the alphabet above the board and on desks
The HWT Aa Bb Cc Print Display Cards are plain and suitable for all grades. The letters are the same as the ones you're teaching. Many teachers also like to give each child one of the HWT Alphabet Desk Strips for easy reference.

Furniture size
Does the furniture fit? The right size and style chair and desk affect school performance. Children don't come in a standard size! One size chair will not fit every child. Check that every child can sit with feet flat on the floor and arms resting comfortably on the desk.

When teaching one-on-one
Be sure to place the right-handed child on your right side. Place the left-handed child on your left side. That way you'll be able to clearly see how the child is writing. When you demonstrate be sure that your hand doesn't hide what you're writing.

Good Posture Can Be Fun

Arms and hands
Here are some warm-ups that children enjoy.

Push palms

Pull hands

Hug yourself tightly

Total posture—Stomp!
Stomping is fun and really works! Sit down and show the children how to stomp their feet and wave their arms in the air. Have them shout, "Na, na, naaah, na, na, naaah," with you while waving and stomping. Nothing's better for getting them to sit correctly. Their feet will be on the floor and parallel in front of them. The arm movements make their trunks straight. The noise and chaos lets them release energy, but it's totally under your control. When you have them stop stomping, they'll have good posture and be ready to pay attention. Use stomping a few times a day.

Head and shoulders
Do this anytime you find your children sagging.

Raise shoulders up

Pull shoulders back

Let them down

Place the Paper

Where's the paper? Most children naturally move a bowl of ice cream to be right in front of them. But, they may lean way over in awkward positions to write. So you need to teach them to place the paper.

Left-handed:

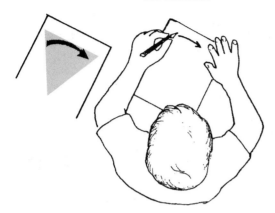

Right-handed:

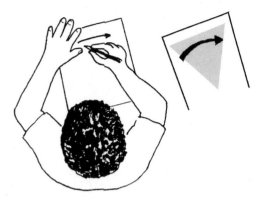

Beginners who are learning to print letters and words should place the paper straight in front of them. Children who are able to print sentences across the page should place the paper at a slight angle to follow the natural arc of the writing hand.

The correct way to tilt the paper is easy to remember (see illustration). For right-handed children, put the right corner higher; for left-handed, the left corner is higher. The writing hand is below the line of writing. This encourages the correct neutral wrist position.

Helping Hand

Where is the "helping hand"—the hand that isn't holding the pencil? I've seen helping hands in laps, twirling hair, or propping up foreheads. So have you! You can nag the child but you'll get better results if you talk directly to the hand! Try it! Take the child's helping hand in yours and pretend to talk to that hand.

Name the helping hand. For example: You have a student named John. Ask John what other name he likes that starts with J. If John says "Jeremy," tell him that you are going to name his helping hand "Jeremy." Have a little talk with "Jeremy" (the helping hand). Tell "Jeremy" that he's supposed to help by holding the paper. Say that John is working really hard on his handwriting, but he needs "Jeremy's" help. Show "Jeremy" where he's supposed to be. Tell John that he might have to remind "Jeremy" about his job.

Kids think this is a hoot. They don't get embarrassed because it's the helping hand, not them, who's being corrected. It's not John who needs to improve, it's "Jeremy." This is a face-saving but effective reminder. One teacher in Wyoming had all her students name their helping hands and even gave them little rings with eyes to wear on the helping hands. The children thought it was fun to tell the helping hand what to do.

Flat fingers please! A flat (but not stiff) helping hand promotes relaxed writing. Put your hand flat on a table and try to feel tension—there isn't any. Make a fist and feel the tension! Children can get uptight while writing, but a flat helping hand decreases tension.

Hold the Pencil

You can put an end to awkward or even fisted pencil grips. Using these tips, your students will hold the pencil with the right combination of mobility and control. Children are "plastic"—they can be molded gently into good habits. These make it easy and fun for children to learn a correct pencil grip.

A-OK

Teach children how to hold the pencil correctly. This is the A-OK way to help children.
The pencil is pinched between the thumb pad and the index finger pad. The pencil rests on the middle finger.

Right-handed:

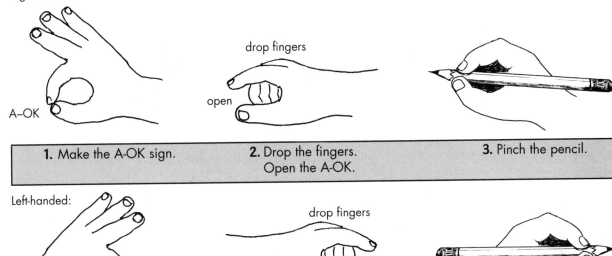

| 1. Make the A-OK sign. | 2. Drop the fingers. Open the A-OK. | 3. Pinch the pencil. |

Left-handed:

Alternate grip

A good alternate grip is a pinch with the thumb and two fingers. The pencil rests on the ring finger.

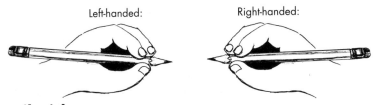

Left-handed: Right-handed:

Flip the pencil trick

Here is another method. It is a trick that someone (in Buffalo, I think) showed me and I've found it so effective and so much fun I've been sharing it ever since. Children like to do it and it puts the pencil in the correct position. (Illustrated for right-handed students.)

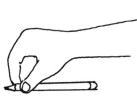

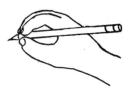

Place pencil on table pointing away from you. Pinch pencil and pick it up. Pinch the pencil where you should hold it—on the paint where the paint meets the wood.

Hold the eraser and twirl it around.

Voila!

Teach the correct pencil grip in three easy steps

This step-by-step technique is a great way to develop a correct pencil grip or to fix awkward ones. The trick is that you don't teach the grip and writing with the grip in the same teaching session. Separate the teaching into these three stages and you will be impressed with how easy the correct grip becomes.

Pick up—Have the child pick up the pencil and hold it in the air with the fingers and thumb correctly placed. Help position the child's fingers if necessary. Tell your students, "Wow that is a perfect pencil grip. Now make a few circles in the air with that perfect pencil grip." Don't let the students write on paper. Just have them pick the pencil up correctly, wave it in the air and gently drop it down. Do this for a few days, until the students can automatically pick up and hold the pencil correctly.

Scribble-wiggle—Give each student a piece of paper with a dot (about three times the size of a period) in the center of the paper. Have the students pick up the pencil, hold it correctly, and put the pencil point on the dot. The little finger side of the "pencil hand" rests on the paper. The child makes wiggly marks through and around the dot without lifting the pencil or hand. (The "helping hand" is flat and holds the paper.) The advantage of this step is that children develop their pencil grip and finger control without being critical of how the writing looks.

Write—Have each student pick up the pencil, hold it correctly and write the first letter of his/her name. Add letters until the children can write their names easily with the correct grip. This will get your students off to a wonderful start. When helping students with poor pencil grips, only insist that they use their new correct grip for writing their names. This will give them frequent practice with the new correct grip. Then slowly build the amount of work that they must do with the new correct grip.

Using pencil grips

If a child continues to have difficulty holding the pencil, there are a variety of grips available at school supply stores, art/stationery stores and catalogs. Their usefulness varies from grip to grip and child to child. Experiment with them and use them only if they make it easier for the child to hold the pencil correctly.

Rubber band trick

Check the angle of the pencil. If it's standing straight up, the pencil will be hard to hold and will cause tension in the fingertips. Put a rubber band around child's wrist. Loop another rubber band to the first one. Pull the loop over to catch the pencil eraser. This may keep the pencil pulled back at the correct angle. If so, you may make or buy a more comfortable version that uses pony tail holders.

Pencil driving tip

Name the fingers: The thumb is the "Dad," the index finger is the "Mom." The remaining fingers are the child and any brothers, sisters, friends, or pets. (Use driver and passenger names to suit child's family.) Say the pencil is the car. Just like in a real car, Dad and Mom sit in front and the kids, friends, or pets sit in back. For safe driving, Dad and Mom face forward (toward the point of the pencil). Dad shouldn't sit on Mom's lap (thumb on top of index finger) and Mom shouldn't sit on Dad's lap (index finger on top of thumb)! If children use an overlapping or tucked-in thumb, remind them that no one can sit on anyone's lap while driving! This is a summary of a tip from Betsy Daniels, COTA/L, and Christine Bradshaw, OTR/L. Betsy's daughter did the illustration (copyrighted and used with permission).

14

Capital Letters Made Easy

My Printing Book and *Printing Power* begin with a quick review of HWT capital letters in special HWT gray blocks. We start with capitals because we expect children already know them. For those who don't, capitals are easy to learn.

Your students will learn to:
- Start capitals at the top.
- Use the correct stroke sequence to form the letters.
- Place all capitals correctly without reversals.

Our unique teaching strategies will help you teach:
- Correct habits for capital letter formation.
- Capital letter recognition.
- Alphabetical order.
- Names and sounds of the letters.
- Classroom social skills.

HWT Letter Style

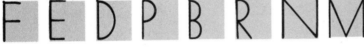

HWT uses a simple, vertical style of printing. Four basic shapes are used to write all of the HWT capital letters. We call the shapes or strokes **big line, little line, big curve, and little curve.** These shapes are familiar to the children who learned with the HWT Capital Letter Wood Pieces and the HWT Slate Chalkboard.

Teaching Order

For capitals, the teaching order is determined by where the letters start and how they are made. Letters that start with the same stroke or in the same place are grouped together.

Frog Jump Capitals

F E D P B R N M

These are the Frog Jump Capitals. They start in the starting corner (top left) with a big line down, and then frog jump back to the starting corner to complete the letter.

Starting Corner Capitals

H K L — H, K, and L start in the starting corner with a big line down.

U V W X Y Z — U, V, W, X, Y, and Z start in the starting corner but then use different strokes to finish the letter.

Center Starters

C O Q G — C, O, Q, and G start with a "Magic C" stroke.

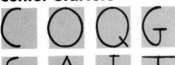

S A I T J — S, A, I, T, and J start at the top center but then use different strokes to finish the letter.

Product and Workbook Design

Teaching Capitals in Kindergarten

The first and second grade workbooks have been designed to provide a brief review of capitals. Children who have used HWT in kindergarten have benefited from unique "no paper, no pencil" techniques to learn capital letters. In kindergarten, children use the HWT Capital Letter Wood Pieces to learn letter formation. They make letters on the HWT Capital Letter Cards and the HWT Mat. The teacher helps children choose the pieces and place them in the correct order and position. Children use the HWT Slate Chalkboard (an old fashioned slate) to write capital letters. Like the mat, the slate has a smiley face in the top left corner. Step by step, each letter is made correctly without reversals.

Wood Pieces Set

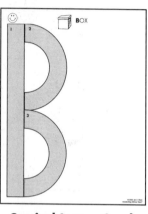
Capital Letter Card

HWT Mat

HWT Slate

Reviewing Capitals in Grades 1 and 2

We review all capital letters in special gray blocks. Gray blocks help children make and place the letters correctly.

Gray blocks help children make letters that begin at the top, use the correct strokes, and are placed correctly—right side up and without reversals. Gray blocks control the size and shape of the letters. Children begin at the top on the dot. The dot in the top left corner (starting corner) is the place to begin F E D P B R N M H K L U V W X Y Z .

The dot in the top center is the place to begin C O Q G S A I T J. Children love to write capitals in the gray blocks. Use gray blocks for review and repair! You can fix all capital problems (reversals, wrong sequence of strokes, or starting at the bottom) with gray blocks.

Reviewing Capitals with Lowercase

Children review the capitals as a group. As each lowercase letter is presented, they review the capital of that letter. Gray blocks are a cue that the letter is a capital. This helps children immediately know which letter is the capital and which is the lowercase letter.

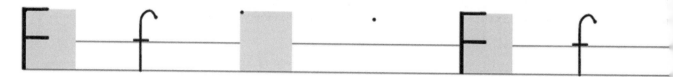

Unique Teaching Strategies

Sign in Please!
You may remember an old TV show where the guests signed in. This adaptation is fun and develops many ABC skills.

Preparation
1. Prepare blackboard with a wide "stop" line near the bottom. (The lesson also works well on whiteboards.)
2. Break chalk into small 1/2" pieces to encourage correct pinch.

Directions
1. Teacher prints A.
   - Write A up high, but reachable for children.
   - Teach A and each letter that follows as you write.
   - Use consistent words as you demonstrate
     (A = big line, big line, and little line).
2. Teacher asks, "Whose name begins with A?" **Adam**!
3. Adam comes to the board and you introduce him
   "This is..... (children say **Adam**)."
   "Adam starts with.....(children say **A**)."
   "In Adam's name, the A makes the
   sound..... (children make the **a sound**)."
4. Adam signs in by making a big line down from
   A. He stops on the line. Continue with each letter.
   Children sign in alphabetically. David is at the
   board now.

What are we learning?
- **Top to bottom** habit.
- **Left to right** sequencing.
- **Stopping** on a line.
- **Correct letter formation**—Children learn by
  watching and hearing the teacher.
- **Pencil grip**—The small pieces of chalk encourage correct grip.
- **Names** of capital letters and classmates.
- **Phonics**—Sounds of letters are easy to do with classmates' names.
- **Alphabetical order**—Children quickly learn their place in the alphabet. They guess which letter is next and watch
  to see if they're right. They look for classmates' names too.
- **Number concepts**—Counting, comparing, and simple charting skills.
- **Big line, little line, big curve, and little curve**—They learn the names for the parts of each letter.
- **Social skills** for school—This is a fun way to learn to listen, be in front of the class, follow directions, and take turns.
  They develop poise and a sense of belonging.

Variation: You can change how children sign in to teach other skills.
- Horizontal line skills—Underline letter from left to right.
- Circle skills—Circle the letter by starting at the top with a C stroke.

Sing "Where Do You Start Your Letters?"
The back of *My Printing Book* and *Printing Power* both have another great way to teach the very important "Start at the top"
habit for capital letters—it's a song. Teach your children the "Where Do You Start Your Letters?" song. Children should know
it so well that they'll sing it at home and in the car. Here's why. The parents listen. The parents learn! Parents are the child's
most important teachers. If parents know that children should start their letters at the top, then they'll model that.

End Reversals with the Mystery Letter Game

Some children reverse capitals or start them from the bottom. The Mystery Letter Game in the workbook will solve both problems. Using the Mystery Letter Game, your children will:

- Begin capital letters at the top.
- Use the correct sequence of strokes.
- Make no reversals!

You can play the Mystery Letter Game with the Frog Jump Capitals. Page 3 of *My Printing Book* and *Printing Power* is designed for the Mystery Letter Game. In the Mystery Letter Game, children start to write a letter but they don't know which letter they are going to make until the teacher tells them. It's a mystery.

This prevents children who have bad habits from using them. If you told the children they were going to make D, some would immediately write D the wrong way. But, because they don't know the name of the letter, they follow the proper formation steps and start developing new habits.

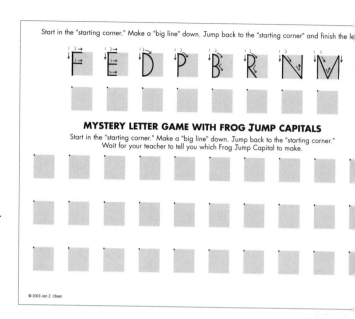

Start in the "starting corner." Make a "big line" down. Jump back to the "starting corner" and finish the le

MYSTERY LETTER GAME WITH FROG JUMP CAPITALS

Start in the "starting corner." Make a "big line" down. Jump back to the "starting corner."
Wait for your teacher to tell you which Frog Jump Capital to make.

© 2003 Jan Z. Olsen

Wet-Dry-Try and the HWT Slate Chalkboard

The HWT slate is used for children who need extra help with learning, forming, or placing capital letters. The frame of the slate controls the size and helps children make straight lines. The smiley face orients children to the top left corner, which prevents reversals.

Teacher's Part

DEMONSTRATE

Demonstrate correct letter formation.

Student's Part

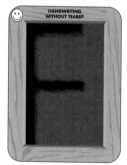

WET

Wet tiny sponge. Squeeze out. With damp sponge, trace over the letter like the teacher demonstrated. Wet index finger. Trace letter again with your wet finger.

DRY

Use a small piece of paper towel to trace the letter dry. Repeat two or three times.

TRY

Now, try writing the letter with a small piece of chalk.

Tips

- Use consistent words to describe the strokes (big line, little line, big curve, little curve).
- Use very small pieces of sponge and chalk—this helps develop the pencil grip.
- Squeeze the sponge well or the letter will be too wet.
- This works best one-on-one or in centers with five or fewer students.
- To use this activity with the whole class you must pre-mark each student slate with the capital letter (so they have a correct model to wet) and then demonstrate once for everyone.

Teaching FROG JUMP CAPITALS

TEACHING ORDER
F E D P B R N M
H K L
U V W X Y Z
C O Q G
S A I T J

My Printing Book and *Printing Power*
pages 2 and 3

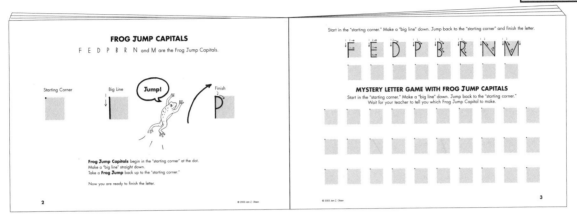

Lesson Plan

Demonstrate F E D P B R N M
Show children how to make F E D P B R N M on the slate and/or in the workbook.
Say the step-by-step directions as you demonstrate.

Teach in workbook
1. Find each capital in the top gray blocks.
2. Copy the capitals in the gray bocks below.
3. Begin on the dot. Follow the directions below for each letter.

Eight capitals are frog jump capitals.

F big line down, Frog Jump! little line across top, little line across middle.
E big line down, Frog Jump! little line across top, middle, bottom.
D big line down, Frog Jump! big curve to bottom corner.
P big line down, Frog Jump! little curve to middle.
B big line down, Frog Jump! little curve to middle, little curve to bottom.
R big line down, Frog Jump! little curve to middle, little line slides to bottom.
N big line down, Frog Jump! big line slides to bottom, big line goes up.
M big line down, Frog Jump! big lines slide down, up, and down.

4. Teach children to play the Mystery Letter Game for Frog Jump Capitals.
• Wait for all students to put pencils on the dot.
• Say, "Make a starting line down, then frog jump back to the top."
• Then say, "Now make a __." Choose a letter: F E D P B R N M.

Tips
• Encourage the student to say the directions out loud. Children like to say "Ribbit" for the frog jump.
• If teaching a class, hold your slate up to demonstrate. Have students imitate on their slates.
• Notice that when the starting line is on the left edge of the slate, the next part of the letter must be placed on the right side. That's right! It is correct and it is on the right-hand side.

Evaluate
• If student makes reversals or starts at the bottom:
  Play the Mystery Letter Game for Frog Jump Capitals.
• If student can't remember the letters:
  Do the slate Wet–Dry–Try activity described on page 18.

19

Teaching
STARTING CORNER CAPITALS

My Printing Book and *Printing Power* – page 4

TEACHING ORDER
F E D P B R N M
H K L
U V W X Y Z
C O Q G
S A I T J

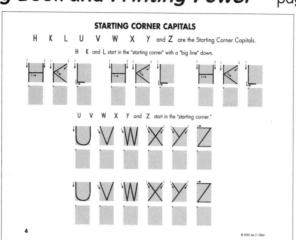

Lesson Plan

Demonstrate H K L U V W X Y Z

Show children how to make H K L U V W X Y Z on the slate and/or in the workbook.
Say the step-by-step directions as you demonstrate.

Teach in workbook

1. Find each capital in the top gray blocks.
2. Copy the capitals in the gray bocks below.
3. Begin on the dot. Follow the directions below for each letter.

Three capitals begin in the starting corner, with a starting line down.

H big line down, big line down, little line across!
(Lefties may make the little line for H like this ⟵ , from right to left.)

K big line down. Lift pencil to top right corner, kick to middle! Slide away.
Children love this story for K: The karate teachers are going to demonstrate. This is Mr. Kaye, a karate teacher. (Put pencil in starting corner. Make big line down.) This is Mrs. Kelly. She is a karate teacher too. (Put pencil in top right corner.) Mrs. Kelly kicks Mr. Kaye right in the middle. Hi...Yaaa! (Make a karate kick with the pencil.)

L big line down, little line across. (Do not pick up the pencil.)

Look! The six capitals at the end of the alphabet all start in the starting corner.

U down, travel, and up.
V big line slides down and up.
W big line slides down and up, down and up.
X big line slides down, big line slides down.
Y little line slides down to middle, big line slides down.
Z across, big line slides down, across.

Tips

• Choose—If you prefer to use an alternate style for Y, that's fine. HWT prefers Y because it uses the same strokes for both the capital and lowercase letter.

Evaluate

• If student has trouble writing diagonal lines:
Give extra help to children who find diagonals difficult. Try the slate strategies. Teach diagonals in other ways by having children play with blocks, ramps, and slides. Use the slate Wet–Dry–Try activity described on page 18.

20

Teaching CENTER STARTERS

TEACHING ORDER
F E D P B R N M
H K L
U V W X Y Z
C O Q G
S A I T J

My Printing Book and *Printing Power* - page 5

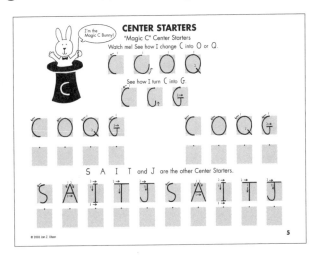

Lesson Plan

Demonstrate C O Q G S A I T J
Show children how to make C O Q G S A I T J on the slate and/or in the workbook.
Say the step-by-step directions as you demonstrate.

Teach in workbook
1. Find each capital in the top gray blocks.
2. Copy the capitals in the gray bocks below.
3. Begin on the dot. Follow the directions below for each letter.

Nine capitals begin at the top center. Letters C O Q G begin with a "Magic C".
C Make a "Magic C".
O Make a "Magic C". Keep on going around. Stop at the top.
Q Make a "Magic C". Keep on going around. Stop at the top. Add a little line.
G Make a "Magic C". Go up. Add a little line.

S Make a little curve (Little "Magic c"). Turn. Make another little curve.
A Big line slides down, big line slides down, little line across.
   (Lefties may do it this way ←—.)
I Big line down, little line across top, little line across bottom.
   (Lefties may do it this way ←—.)
T Big line down, little line across top. (Lefties may do it this way ←—.)
J Big line down, turn, stop; little line across top. (Lefties may do it this way ←—.)

Tips
• One side of the slate has the words "Handwriting Without Tears®" at the top center.
  Use this side to help children find the center.

Evaluate
• If there are C problems:
  Use the slate. Start in the center and then go toward the smiley face. Tell children to
  say "Hello" to the smiley face, but don't stay!
• If there are S problems:
  If children get stuck after the first little curve, tell them to "Stop, drop, and roll." Or
  try the slate Wet–Dry–Try activity described on page 18.
• If there are J problems:
  Use the slate. "Big line down, turn toward the smiley face side of the slate."

Lowercase Letters Made Easy

The purpose of *My Printing Book* and *Printing Power* is to enable all children to print with speed, neatness, and confidence. In the next few pages you will see how the HWT letter style, teaching order, workbook design, and unique teaching strategies make it easy for your students to succeed.

HWT Letter Style

a b c d e f g h i j k l m n o p q r s t u v w x y z

HWT uses a simple, continuous-stroke, vertical style. The vertical style is easy for children to learn. The HWT letter style is also familiar to them because it looks the same as the letters and words they see in their daily life. HWT's continuous-stroke style prevents reversals and prepares children for cursive.

Teaching Order

The teaching order for HWT lowercase letters is based on:
- Complexity of the letter—Letters that are easy to form or like the capital are taught earlier.
- Formation patterns—Letters that use the same strokes are generally grouped together.
- Frequency of use—This was determined by counting letters in the Dolch word lists for Grades K , 1, and 2. The frequency of letter use order is:

    e o a t n s h i l r w u d y m f k g b p c v j q z x

- Possibility of reversal—Letters that children may confuse (b and d and g, q, and p) are separated by many pages.

c o s v w — We start with c o s v w because they are easy—they are the same as their capital partners, just smaller. They all start on the top line and fit between the HWT double lines.

t — Lowercase t is like capital T, but is crossed lower. This is the first letter children learn that starts above the double lines.

a d g — The "Magic c" letters, a d and g, all begin with a c stroke. They are also frequently used letters.

u i e — These letters complete the vowels. Letter e is difficult to write, but is the most frequently used letter.

l k y j — This is a transition group. Letters l and k begin above the HWT double lines, and y and j descend below.

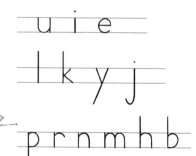

p r n m h b — The diver letters, p r n m h and b, use a similar stroke pattern: "dive down, come up, and swim over to the right." We avoid b and d confusion by separating these letters by many pages. Further, by teaching b after h, children will write b using the correct stroke order.

f q x z — This is the final group. Letter f is taught here because it has a difficult starting stroke. Letter q is taught here to avoid confusion with g. Letters x and z are capital partners but are introduced last because of their infrequent use.

Workbook Design

Huge Step-by-Step Illustrated Directions

To really understand correct letter formation, children need to see each step in sequence. Tiny direction arrows on a picture of a finished letter simply won't do! In the HWT workbook letter demonstrations, each step is large enough to finger trace. Finger tracing helps children learn through their tactile (touch) and kinesthetic (movement) senses.

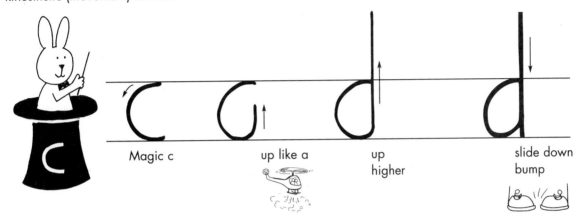

Magic c   up like a   up higher   slide down bump

Child-Friendly, Consistent Terminology

The workbooks use child-friendly words to describe each step for making the letters. Students will know what you mean when you say "Magic "c," up, up like a helicopter, slide down, bump." There is no strange jargon or indecipherable terminology. The books are for children and use language and symbols that they understand. Read the directions out loud to the students. This helps your auditory (hearing) learners remember how to form the letters correctly.

HWT Double Lines

The HWT workbooks use double guidelines. The bottom line keeps the writing straight and the top line controls the size. The double lines end the problem of line confusion. Trying to follow typical beginner lined paper is like learning to drive on a four lane freeway—a blue line at the top, a dotted line in the middle, a red line on the bottom, and another blue line below. It is easy to understand why so many children have trouble.

Just two lines are easy. On the HWT double lines many letters fit exactly between the double lines and most letters (19 out of 26!) begin exactly on the top line. The children find it easy to notice and place the letters that go above the lines and the letters that go below. They have more control, confidence, and size consistency using HWT double lines.

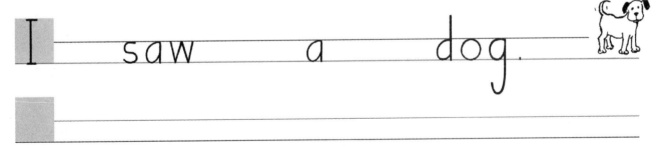

Fair Practice

In the workbooks, we never ask the child to copy or use a letter that has not been taught. The words and sentences use only the letters that the children already know. Other workbooks give word and sentence writing practice that includes letters that the children haven't learned yet. This isn't fair and often causes children to develop bad habits.

Copy One Time Only from Each Model

Practice can make a child's writing worse. Have you seen papers or workbooks where the children are supposed to copy a letter over and over across the page? The child copies the model and then copies the copy of the model, and so on. The letters get progressively worse. It's boring. It's much better to have the child make just one letter beside each model.

When practicing words, children write each word once beside the model.

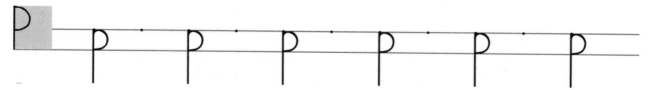

Continuous Meaningful Review

Children retain skills better if they have continuous meaningful review. That's why we put each new letter into meaningful use in words and sentences. The words and sentences emphasize practice of the new letter while reviewing previously learned letters. Special letter review pages also give practice for specific letter groups.

Room to Write

When children are learning to print, they need extra room to write. Only HWT workbooks give children enough room to write. Other workbooks give one spacebar space between words. But children can't print with the precision of machines! So they end up cramming theirwordstogether to make them fit.

The HWT workbooks give generous spaces after words. It's easy for children to see the spaces between words. There's plenty of room in "first class" for children to write and have space between words! This generous spacing teaches good spacing habits for words and sentences.

Copy directly under each word.

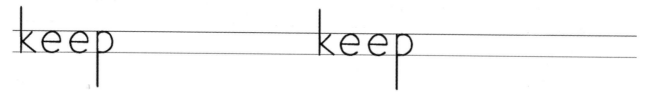

Left-Hand Friendly Design

The HWT workbooks are left-hand friendly. Every page is designed with the models positioned so that the left-handed child can easily see the model they are copying. Left-handers never have to lift their hand or place their hand in an awkward position to see a model.

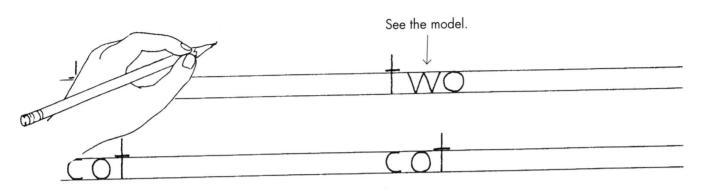

See the model.

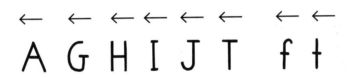

A G H I J T f t

Special exception: Left-handed people naturally make horizontal lines from right to left, pulling into the hand. Make sure you do not correct this as it is natural and not a problem. But for E, F, and L we suggest all children push off from the big line using a left to right stroke.

Simple Black-and-White Pages

The HWT workbooks have black-and-white pages that are clean and clear. We deliberately avoid the visual confusion of distracting background images, overdone colored graphics, multicolored lines, and crowded pages. These "fancy" effects can create visual perceptual difficulties for children and distract them.

The simple workbook pages keep children happy and occupied. The children who finish first can color the pictures or add drawings to the pages.

Children enjoy seeing their own writing and coloring or drawing on the pages. They like that the models are handwritten. Their writing looks like the writing in the book. HWT workbooks celebrate the child's work.

Left-to-Right Directionality

This is an exciting, unique feature of the HWT workbooks. Look at our illustrations! They promote left-to-right directionality. The alligator, cow, tow truck, and other drawings are going from left to right across the page to encourage correct visual tracking and writing from left to right on the page.

Unique Teaching Strategies

Magic c, up like a helicopter, slide down, bump

Demonstrate with Voices at the Blackboard

Prepare
1. Premark the double lines on the chalkboard.
2. Begin at the far left of the board.
3. Have the students open their workbooks, find the step-by-step directions, and read the words out loud with them.

Demonstrate
1. Demonstrate the letter, describing each step.
2. Say the words that are in the workbook.
3. Ask the children to say the words with you.

Demonstrate Again and Again, But Never Bore Them!
1. Demonstrate the letter and say the words with **high** voices.
2. Demonstrate the letter and say the words with **low** voices.
3. Demonstrate the letter and say the words with **loud** voices.
4. Demonstrate the letter and say the words with **soft** voices.
5. Demonstrate the letter and say the words with **slow** voices.
6. Demonstrate the letter and say the words with **fast** voices.

Results
1. Your children will know how to make each part of the letter.
2. They will memorize the words for each step.
3. They will be able to talk themselves through making the letter.

Student Participation with Wet-Dry-Try

Bring your students up to the board to trace over the letters you have made. It's teacher's choice how you do this. You may simply have them finger trace over the letters. Or you may have a dish of small damp sponges and let the first groups wet the letters. The next group can dry, and the last group can try writing the letters with chalk. You may also invite children to student teach at the board under your supervision. One way to do this is to ask children who have the letter in their name to help teach.

Demonstrate

The teacher teaches the letter by demonstration and describing each step.

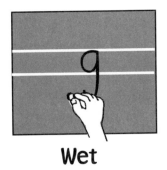

Wet

Wet the teacher's chalk letter by tracing over it with a tiny wet sponge.

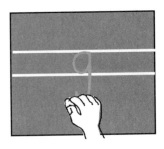

Dry

Dry the letter with a piece of paper towel.

Try

Try writing the letter with chalk.

Demonstrate at the Whiteboard

If you have whiteboards you will demonstrate there. While you won't be able to use the Wet–Dry–Try technique, you can have children erase with a tissue to give them the opportunity to write large on a vertical surface.

Demonstrate in the Workbooks

Some children also need to see you write in their workbooks. Demonstrate the letter once for them and then have them make one for you. After you watch, you'll know if they need help and where. A few children need to watch more than once. Demonstrate the letter two times. Then ask, "Do you want to see it again before you try?" Children are so savvy about knowing how many times they need to see it. Let them tell you.

Pleasing Practice

Children love the short practice! The focus is always on using correct habits and doing one's best work, not on finishing a page! Lessons are about 10 minutes a day with just 5 minutes of actual practice time. The focus of our practice is on the process, not the product. With correct practice, the product will naturally improve. The teacher must be sure that the child is practicing the correct habits.

Teaching c o s v w

Key Points: Children learn that lowercase c o s v w are the same as C O S V W, just lower. They place the lowercase letters on the double lines.

Grade 2 – *Printing Power* – page 8

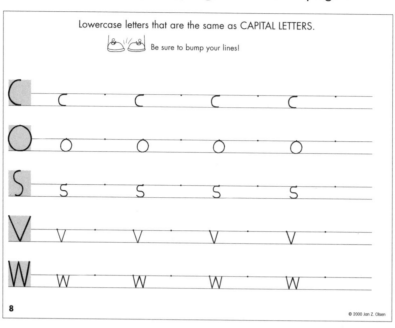

Lowercase letters that are the same as CAPITAL LETTERS.
Be sure to bump your lines!

8   © 2000 Jan Z. Olsen

Note: *Printing Power* has c o s v w on one page. *My Printing Book* has a separate page for each letter. Teachers working with *My Printing Book* should go on to the next five pages in this guide for the lesson plans for each individual letter. Teachers using *Printing Power* should review this page and then skip to page 34 in this guide.

Lesson Plan

Demonstrate c o s v w

Show children how to make c o s v w on the board and/or in the workbook. Say the step-by-step directions as you demonstrate.

Teach in workbook

1. Find each capital C O S V W on the gray block.
2. Find the lowercase partner on the double lines next to it.
3. Copy the lowercase letters. Teacher should demonstrate, coach, and watch students.
Note: Tell left-handed students to copy from the model on the right.

Tips

- Teach that the capital and lowercase letters are the same, but lowercase letters are lower.
- Teach students to start exactly on the dot on the line.
- Emphasize "bumping" or touching the bottom line.

Evaluate

- If letters are reversed and aren't started at the top, use the slate and the Wet–Dry–Try method described on page 18.

✓ **Check your teaching with __cows__**
This simple check up will tell you if your student has mastered the lessons so far. On a blank piece of paper, draw a single line. Ask the child to print the word "cows" on the line. Spell the word out loud for the child, c – o – w – s, and watch how each letter is printed. Did the child begin every letter at the top? Were the letters the same height? Any reversals of c or s? Reteach as needed.

© 2003 Jan Z. Olsen

Teaching c

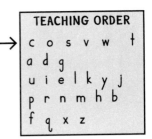

TEACHING ORDER

c o s v w t
a d g
u i e l k y j
p r n m h b
f q x z

Key Points: Children learn to place lowercase c on the double lines. Starting c at the top is a critical habit not just for c, but for a d g o (and later q), all of which begin with a c stroke. The next five pages are all from Grade 1, *My Printing Book.*

Grade 1 - *My Printing Book -* page 7

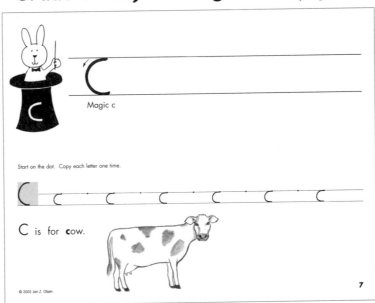

Magic c

Start on the dot. Copy each letter one time.

C is for **c**ow.

© 2003 Jan Z. Olsen   7

Lesson Plan

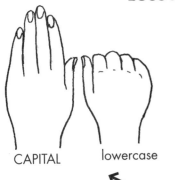

CAPITAL   lowercase

Demonstrate c

Show children how to make c on the board and/or in the workbook.
Start at the top. Make a c stroke. Say the words "Magic c."

Teach in workbook

1. Find the picture of the Magic C Bunny.
Read "Magic c."
Finger trace the huge c.
2. Find C on the gray block and c on the double lines.
Copy c's. Teacher should demonstrate, coach, and watch students.
3. Read "C is for cow." Move finger under the sentence from left to right.
Find C and c in the sentence. Color the cow and draw grass for the cow.

Tips

* Teach that C and c are the same, but c is lower.
* To emphasize the difference between C and c:
Hold up your left hand flat and say, "This is capital C." Hold right hand up fisted.
Put it next to your left thumb. Say, "This is lowercase c. It's lower!"
* Teach left-handed students to copy from the model on the right.

Evaluate

* If c is too skinny:
Start on the dot and then travel on the top line before curving down.
This will make for a bigger curve.
* If c is reversed:
Teach C on the slate. Start in the top center and move chalk toward the ☺ side.
Use the Wet–Dry–Try method described on page 18.

© 2003 Jan Z. Olsen   **29**

Teaching o

Key Points: Begin o with a Magic "c." Letter o is the second most frequently used letter.

TEACHING ORDER

→ c o s v w t
a d g
u i e l k y j
p r n m h b
f q x z

Grade 1 - *My Printing Book* - page 8

Magic c   keep on   stop
                going

Start on the dot. Copy each letter one time.

O is for **o**wl.

8   © 2003 Jan Z. Olsen

Lesson Plan

Demonstrate o

Show children how to make o on the board and/or in the workbook.
Say the step-by-step directions as you demonstrate.

Teach in workbook

1. Find the picture of the Magic C Bunny.
   Read the instructions, "Magic C—keep on going—stop."
   Finger trace the step-by-step models.
2. Find O on the gray block and o on the double lines.
   Copy the o's. Teacher should demonstrate, coach, and watch students.
3. Read "O is for owl." Move finger under the sentence from left to right.
   See how O and o are used in the sentence.
   Children may color the owl or draw other "O" pictures like octopus or orange.

Tips

- Teach that O and o are the same, but o is lower.
- Teach students to start exactly on the dot.

Evaluate

- If letter o doesn't start at the top, or goes the wrong way:
  Use the slate. Start in the top center and move chalk toward the 🙂 in a c stroke.
  Use the Wet–Dry–Try method described on page 18.
- Emphasize "bumping" or touching the bottom line.

30

© 2003 Jan Z. Olsen

Teaching s

TEACHING ORDER

→ c o s v w t
a d g
u i e l k y j
p r n m h b
f q x z

Key Points: Letter s is the sixth most frequently used letter. Careful teaching is very important because s changes direction in the stroke.

Grade 1 - *My Printing Book* - page 9

little Magic c

little curve   turn down   little curve around

Start on the dot. Copy each letter one time.

s   s   S   S   S   S

S is for **s**nowman.

© 2003 Jan Z. Olsen

9

Lesson Plan

Demonstrate S

Show children how to make s on the board and/or in the workbook.
Say the step-by-step directions as you demonstrate.

Teach in workbook

1. Find the little Magic C Bunny.
   Read the instructions, "little curve—turn down—little curve around."
   Finger trace the step-by-step models.
2. Find S on the gray block and s on the double lines.
   Copy the s's. Teacher should demonstrate, coach, and watch students.
3. Read "S is for snowman." Move finger under the sentence from left to right.
   See how S and s are used in the sentence.
   Children may color the scarf and make more snowmen.

HANDWRITING WITHOUT TEARS®

Tip

• Teach that S and s are the same, but s is lower.

Evaluate

• If letter s doesn't start at the top, or goes the wrong way:
  Use the slate. Start at the top center and move chalk toward the ☺ with a little c stroke.
• If the child has problems changing directions for s:
  Use the Wet–Dry–Try method described on page 18.
• If the child gets stuck after the first little curve:
  Tell child to "STOP, DROP, and ROLL."

© 2003 Jan Z. Olsen

31

Teaching v

Key Points: Letter v prepares children to make w correctly. Diagonal letters are difficult.

TEACHING ORDER

c o s v w t
a d g
u i e l k y j
p r n m h b
f q x z

Grade 1 – *My Printing Book* – page 10

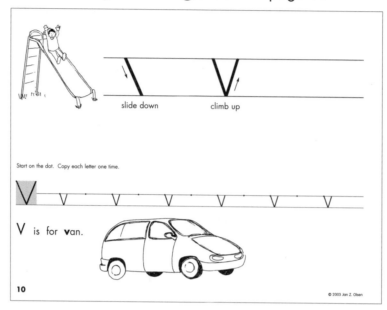

slide down   climb up

Start on the dot. Copy each letter one time.

V is for **v**an.

10

© 2003 Jan Z. Olsen

Lesson Plan

Demonstrate V

Show children how to make v on the board and/or in the workbook.
Say the step-by-step directions as you demonstrate.

Teach in workbook

1. Find the slide.
   Read the instructions, "slide down, climb up."
   Finger trace the step-by-step models.
2. Find V on the gray block and v on the double lines.
   Copy the v's. Teacher should demonstrate, coach, and watch students.
3. Read "V is for van." Move finger under the sentence from left to right.
   See how V and v are used in the sentence.
   Children may color the van.

Tips

- Teach that V and v are the same, but v is lower.
- Show children how to make a V with fingers, and finger trace the "down and up."

Evaluate

- If a child has problems with diagonal lines:
  Teach V on the slate. V starts in the starting corner.
  Use the slate Wet–Dry–Try method described on page 18.
  Use real-life experiences with slides and ramps.

32

© 2003 Jan Z. Olsen

Teaching w

Key Points: Letters v and w use the same down and up stroke pattern. Letter w is the eleventh most frequently used letter.

TEACHING ORDER

c o s v w t
a d g
u i e l k y j
p r n m h b
f q x z

Grade 1 – *My Printing Book* – page 11

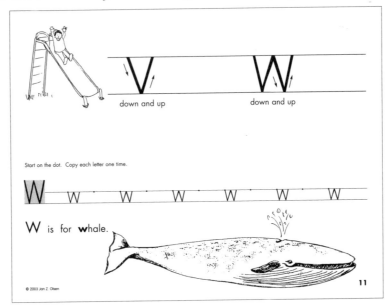

down and up   down and up

Start on the dot. Copy each letter one time.

W W W W W W W

W is for **w**hale.

© 2003 Jan Z. Olsen

11

Lesson Plan

Demonstrate W

Show children how to make w on the board and/or in the workbook.
Say the step-by-step directions as you demonstrate.

Teach in workbook

1. Find the slide.
   Read the instructions, "down and up . . . down and up."
   Finger trace the step-by-step models.
2. Find W on the gray block and w on the double lines.
   Copy the w's. Teacher should demonstrate, coach, and watch students.
3. Read "W is for whale." Move finger under the sentence from left to right.
   See how W and w are used in the sentence.

Tips

- Teach that W and w are the same, but w is lower.
- Emphasize "bumping" the lines.

Note: Use the slate only for capital letters! If the lowercase letter is the same as the capital, then of course you may use the slate. Children love the slate activities and they are helpful for teaching correct letter formation.

Evaluate

- If a child has problems with diagonal lines:
  Teach W on the slate. W starts in the starting corner. Use the slate Wet–Dry–Try method described on page 18.
  Use real-life experiences with slides and ramps.

✓ **Check your teaching with __cows__**
This simple checkup will tell you if your student has mastered the lessons. On a blank piece of paper, draw a single line. Ask the child to print the word "cows" on the line. Spell the word out loud for the child, c—o—w—s, and watch how each letter is printed. Did the child begin every letter at the top? Were the letters the same height? Any reversals of c or s? Reteach as needed.

© 2003 Jan Z. Olsen

33

Teaching †

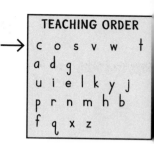

TEACHING ORDER

c o s v w t
a d g
u i e l k y j
p r n m h b
f q x z

Key Points: Lowercase t is the first letter that starts above the double lines.
Letter t is the fourth most frequently used letter.

Grade 1 - *My Printing Book*
page 12

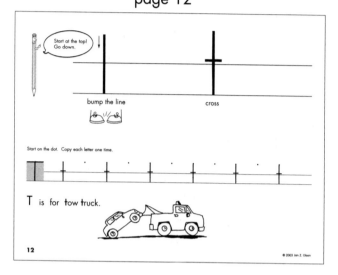

Grade 2 - *Printing Power*
page 9

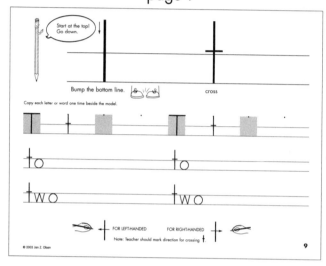

Extra: Read "T is for tow truck." Move finger under the sentence from left to right. Students may color the picture.

Lesson Plan

Demonstrate †

Show children how to make t on the board and/or in the workbook.
Say the step-by-step directions as you demonstrate.

Teach in workbook

1. Read the directions.
   Finger trace the step-by-step models.
2. Find T on the gray block and t on the double lines.
   Copy the letters. Teacher should demonstrate, coach, and watch students.
3. Copy the word lists. See following page for tips on word lists.

Tips

- Teach that T and t are the same height. Both start above the lines. Lowercase t is just crossed lower.
- Show children how to make T with hands. Then lower the hand to make lowercase t. Say T and t are both tall, but lowercase t is crossed lower.
- Children cross t according to their handedness.
  Teacher marks arrow ⟶ on cross for right-handed students.
  Teacher marks arrow ⟵ on cross for left-handed students.

Evaluate

- If t is too short:
  Make T and t with hands. Both are tall. Say t is tall like a teenager and is allowed to start higher.

34

Teaching with Twin Word Lists

Key Points: The list of words on the left has a twin list in the middle of the page. These words only use letters that the children have been taught. Copy each word one time beside the model. Left-handed students look on the middle column when they copy.

Grade 1 - *My Printing Book*
page 13

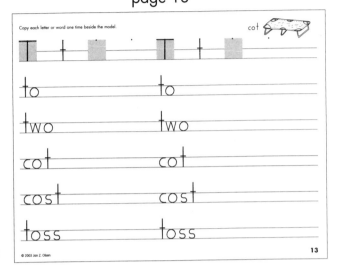

Grade 2 - *Printing Power*
page 9

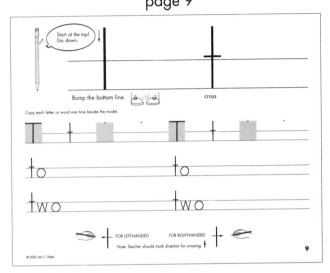

Lesson Plan

Demonstrate each word on the board
Show children how to print each word on the board and/or in the workbook. Describe each letter as you write.

Teach in workbook
1. Show the Twin word lists. Ask, "Are they the same or different?" The same!
2. Students leave a space before beginning to copy words.
3. Students copy words from left to right. Grade 1 teachers may assign just half the page (one list) now and let students finish the other column later.

Tips
- Students copy each list one time. (Help left-handed students to look at the middle list.) You can choose how to use the letter and word list pages.
- Do you want to teach all the letters quickly? Then go through the whole book using just the letters and one or two words. Then start over and work slowly through the book.
- Do you want to reduce work for some students? Assign half the work—tell them to copy just one list.

Evaluate

- If some letters are too far apart:
  Teach your students to put letters in a word close to each other. Have them put their index fingers up and bring them close together, without touching. Tell them, "In a word, the letters are close, but don't touch." Draw fingers for them!
- If some letters are not placed correctly on the lines:
  Teach that c o s v w are the same height and fit between the double lines. Letter t should stick out because it starts higher.
- If some letters are made from the bottom:
  Teach that no letters ever begin on the bottom line.

35

Meet the Magic c Bunny!

- The Magic c Bunny changes letter c into new letters. That's the magic trick!

- You may purchase a puppet from HWT. See page 1 for a photo of the puppet.

- You may follow the directions below to make a Magic c Bunny from a napkin.

I'm the Magic c Bunny

Make a Magic c Bunny!

1

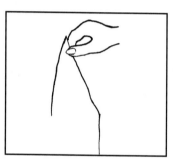

Open paper napkin. Hold by one corner.

2

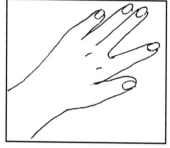

Spread index and middle fingers apart.

3

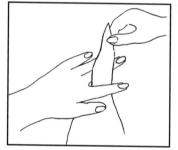

Pull corner between your index and middle fingers. (First ear!)

4

Take the next corner. Pull corner between your middle and ring fingers. (Second ear!)

5

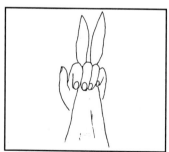

Fold fingers into palm.

6

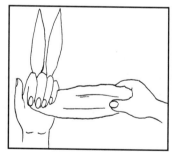

Pull napkin out to side.

7

Wrap napkin over fingers and tuck into hand.

8

Add the face with a pen. It's a bunny! You may slip the bunny off your fingers and give it to a child. Tape or staple the napkin to hold it.

Teaching *a*

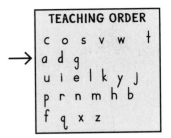

TEACHING ORDER

c o s v w t
a d g
u i e l k y j
p r n m h b
f q x z

Key Points: Letter a is the third most frequently used letter. Letter a begins on the top with a "Magic c" stroke. It is made in a continuous stroke.

Grade 1 – *My Printing Book*
page 14

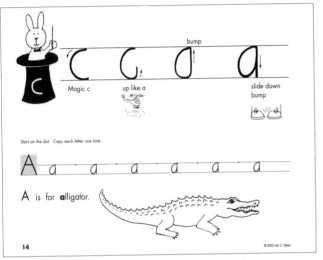

Grade 2 – *Printing Power*
page 10

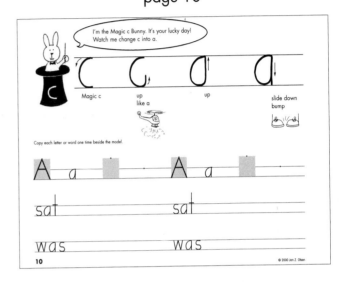

Extra: Read "A is for alligator." Move finger under the sentence from left to right. Students may color the alligator or draw pictures of things that begin with a (apple, arrow, ant).

Lesson Plan

Demonstrate *a*
Show children how to make a on the board and/or in the workbook.
Say the step-by-step directions as you demonstrate.

Teach in workbook
1. Read the directions.
   Finger trace the step-by-step models.
2. Find A on the gray block and a on the double lines.
   Copy the letters. Teacher should demonstrate, coach, and watch students.
3. Copy the word lists. Grade 1 teachers may assign one list now, another later.

Tips
- Teach that A and a are different.

Evaluate
- If a is too skinny:
  Start on the dot and travel on the top line before curving down.
- If child has a bad habit for making a:
  After teaching d and g, use the Mystery Letter Game for "Magic c" letters to correct this habit. See page 40 of this book for directions.

Teaching d

Key Points: Letter d begins on the top line with a "Magic c" stroke. Beginning with a c stroke eliminates reversals and prepares students for cursive. Letter d is used more frequently than b. It is taught separately from b to avoid reversals.

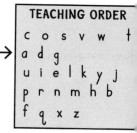

TEACHING ORDER
c o s v w t
a d g
u i e l k y j
p r n m h b
f q x z

Grade 1 – *My Printing Book*
page 16

Extra: Read "D is for duck." Move finger under the sentence from left to right. Students may color the duck or draw pictures of things that begin with d (doll, diamond, donut).

Grade 2 – *Printing Power*
page 11

Lesson Plan

Demonstrate d

Show children how to make d on the board and/or in the workbook. Say the step-by-step directions as you demonstrate.

Teach in workbook

1. Read the directions.
   Finger trace the step-by-step models.
2. Find D on the gray block and d on the double lines.
   Copy the letters. Teacher should demonstrate, coach, and watch students.
3. Copy the word lists. Grade 1 teachers may assign one list now, another later.

Tips

- Teach that D and d are different.
- Teach that d starts with c.
- Say "a b c—see the c change into d!"
- Teach that d goes above the lines.

Evaluate

- If a child doesn't retrace the line down:
  Tell the child to think of sliding down a pole. "Hang on until your feet touch the ground."
- If a child makes a short d:
  Tell the child to go up higher in the helicopter.

38

Teaching g

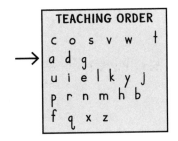

TEACHING ORDER

c o s v w   t
a d g
u i e l k y j
p r n m h b
f q x z

Key Points: Letter g is the first letter to go below the line. Begin with a "Magic c" stroke.

Grade 1 - *My Printing Book*
page 18

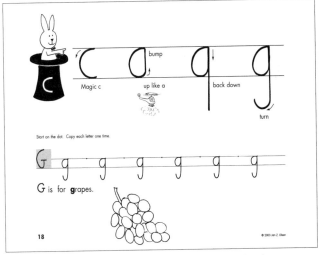

Extra: Read "G is for grapes." Move finger under the sentence from left to right. Students may color the grapes or draw pictures of things that begin with g (grapefruit, goggles, goldfish).

Grade 2 - *Printing Power*
page 12

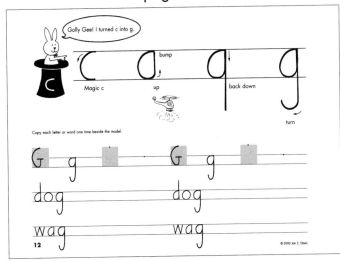

Extra: Page 13 in *Printing Power* has more word practice.

Lesson Plan
Demonstrate g

Show children how to make g on the board and/or in the workbook. Say the step-by-step directions as you demonstrate.

Teach in workbook

1. Read the directions.
   Finger trace the step-by-step models.
2. Find G on the gray block and g on the double lines.
   Copy the letters. Teacher should demonstrate, coach, and watch students.
3. Copy the word lists. Grade 1 teachers may assign one list now, another later.
   Grade 2 students copy words on Practice Page 13.

Tips
- Teach that G and g are different.
- Teach the turn. Draw a little face in the g. That's George. He says "Ooooh! If I fall, will you catch me?" Sure! Turn the g to catch George and it will always be turned the right way.

Evaluate
- If g is floating:
  Tell child to make g go straight down below the line.

✓ **Check your teaching with cat   dog**
On a blank piece of paper, draw a single line. Ask child to print "cat" and "dog" on the line. Spell out c-a-t and d-o-g. Did the child use a c stroke to begin a d g o? Is t taller? Did g go below the line? Reteach as needed. Use the Mystery Letter Game for "Magic c" letters, taught on the following page, to correct c a d g o problems.

39

Mystery!! Mastering "Magic c" Letters!

Key Points: This game promotes correct habits and eliminates bad ones. Children will automatically begin letters a d g o correctly with a "Magic c" stroke.

Grades 1 and 2 – *My Printing Book* and *Printing Power*
page 20 and page 14

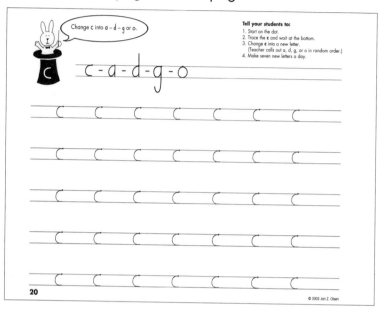

Lesson Plan

Demonstrate "Magic c" letters
Show children how each of the letters begins with c.
The letter c magically changes into a d g or o.

Teach in workbook
Wait for all students to put pencils on the dot. Tell students to:
1. Start on the dot.
2. Trace the c and wait at the bottom.
3. Now change c into a new letter. (Call out a, d, g, or o in random order.)

Tips
- Do not name the letter first. The name of the letter is a secret! If children don't know which letter they are making, they can't use bad habits.
- Complete just one line of letters a day. Spread this activity out over time for best results.
- Repeat the activity as needed until there are no problems with "Magic c" letters.

Evaluate
- Observe your children as they write the c-based letters. Do all begin with a "Magic c" stroke? Continue this game until correct habits are completely automatic. You can check with words like go, coat, and dad.

Teaching Sentence Skills

Key Points: Children learn to begin a sentence with a capital letter, use space between words, and end with a period. Generous spaces give children room to write.

Grade 1 - *My Printing Book*
page 21

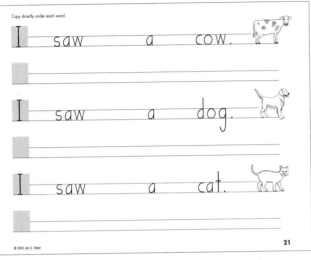

This book uses gray blocks for capitals. Note the generous spaces between words.

Grade 2 - *Printing Power*
page 15

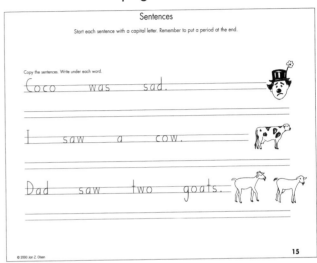

This book is more advanced. It has smaller size printing and more complex sentences.

Lesson Plan

Teach in workbook

1. **Begin sentences with a capital letter.**
   The "A is for alligator" type sentences in *My Printing Book* teach the correct use of A and a. Extra challenge for grade 2: Students must learn to begin the capital letter up high, above the lines.

2. **Leave space between words.**
   Have students copy directly under each word. Both workbooks use generous spaces to give lots of room to write. Exaggerating the spaces now will result in beautiful sentence spacing as a habit.

3. **End with a period.**
   At this point, we are just using periods. Would you like to teach the "?"? Explain that if a sentence asks a question, it ends with a ?. Help them find ? in books, and practice writing a few. Surprise! You may also teach the exclamation point.

Tip

- A sentence expresses a complete thought. Explain the difference between just words (plain, cheese, pepperoni) and a real sentence (I eat pizza.) A sentence has a SUBJECT (who?) and a PREDICATE (did what?).

Evaluate

- If students run their words together:
  Say that you will give them what they need for spaces. Have them hold out their hands to catch it. Take a huge empty bottle (or any container) and make a big show of pouring into their hands. Ask, "What did you get?" Nothing! Tell them to put "nothing" after every word they write.
- Be sure that you use very generous spaces and that any handouts you use give children enough room to write.

Teaching u

Key Point: Letters u i e complete the vowels.

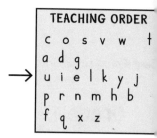

TEACHING ORDER						
c	o	s	v	w	t	
a	d	g				
→ u	i	e	l	k	y	J
p	r	n	m	h	b	
f	q	x	z			

Grade 1 - *My Printing Book*
page 22

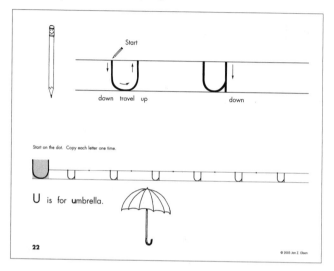

Extra: Read "U is for umbrella." Move finger under the sentence from left to right. Students may color the umbrella and draw more umbrellas.

Grade 2 - *Printing Power*
page 16

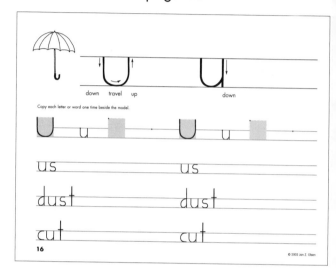

Lesson Plan

Demonstrate U
Show children how to make u on the board and/or in the workbook. Say the step-by-step directions as you demonstrate.

Teach in workbook
1. Read the directions.
   Finger trace the step-by-step models.
2. Find U on the gray block and u on the double lines.
   Copy the letters. Teacher should demonstrate, coach, and watch students.
3. Copy the word lists. Grade 1 teachers may assign one list now, another later.

Tips
- U and u are almost the same. The only difference is the final line down on u.
- Teach careful retracing for line down.

Evaluate
- If u is too pointed like a v:
  Travel on the bottom line. Take at least "two steps" on the line and then come up straight.

42

Teaching i

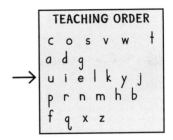

TEACHING ORDER

c o s v w t
a d g
→ u i e l k y j
p r n m h b
f q x z

Key Point: Letter i is the 8th most frequently used letter.

Grade 1 - *My Printing Book*
page 24

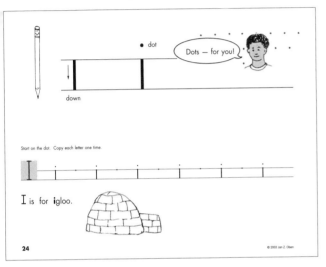

Extra: Read "I is for igloo." Move finger under the sentence from left to right. Students may color the igloo or draw pictures of things that begin with i (insect, iceberg, ice cream).

Grade 2 - *Printing Power*
page 17

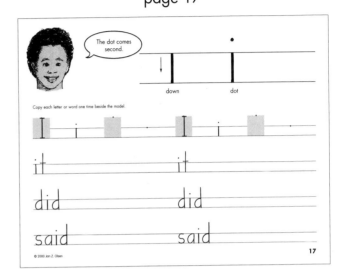

Lesson Plan

Demonstrate i

Show children how to make i on the board and/or in the workbook. Say the step-by-step directions as you demonstrate.

Teach in workbook

1. Read the directions.
   Finger trace the step-by-step models.
2. Find I on the gray block and i on the double lines.
   Copy the letters. Teacher should demonstrate, coach, and watch students.
3. Copy the word lists. Grade 1 teachers may assign one list now, another later.

Tips

- Teach that I and i are different.
- Teach that i is never used alone.
- Teach children to make the line before the dot. Be flexible about what the dots look like. Allow a little creativity.

Evaluate

- If i is too short:
  Tell the child to place the pencil on the top line, then bump the bottom line.
- If the child makes a small circle to dot the i, it's okay. It's a personal style.

Teaching e

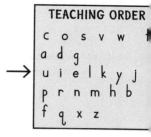

TEACHING ORDER

c o s v w
a d g
u i e l k y j
p r n m h b
f q x z

Key Point: Letter e is the most frequently used letter.

Grade 1 – *My Printing Book*
page 26

Extra: Read "E is for elephant." Move finger under the sentence from left to right. Students may color the elephant or draw pictures of things that begin with e.

Grade 2 – *Printing Power*
page 18

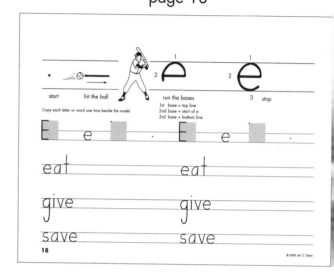

Lesson Plan

Demonstrate e

Show children how to make e on the board and/or in the workbook. Say the step-by-step directions as you demonstrate.

Teach in workbook

1. Read the directions. Start e in the middle, on the dot.
   Finger trace the step-by-step models.
2. Find E on the gray block and e on the double lines.
   Copy the letters. Touch all the bases. Teacher should demonstrate, coach, and watch students.
3. Copy the word lists. Grade 1 teachers may assign one list now, another later.

Tips

- Lowercase e does not begin on a line—it begins in the air between the lines. A visual cue may be needed (a dot) for the child to become comfortable with this.
- Remind the child that it is "not a homerun," so only run to 3rd base!

Evaluate

- If the beginning line isn't straight:
  Have student practice writing straight dashes between the lines.
- For a nice pointed e:
  Emphasize "hit the ball" STRAIGHT, wait, then run the bases.

44

Grade 1 Practice

Key Points: Generous spaces between words give students room to write. Be sure to model generous spaces when you write.

My Printing Book

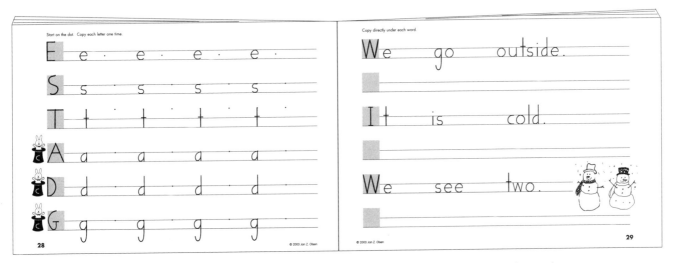

Letter review
page 28

Sentence practice
page 29

- Letter review for e s t a d g.
- Use this page for daily practice.
- Put the pencil on the dot! Do one column a day.
- Demonstrate, coach, and watch students.

- Copy directly under each word.
- Generous spaces give room to write.
- Gray blocks help with capital letter placement.

Second grade teachers, turn the page for your Grade 2 Practice!

Grade 2 Practice

Printing Power

Rhyming practice
page 19

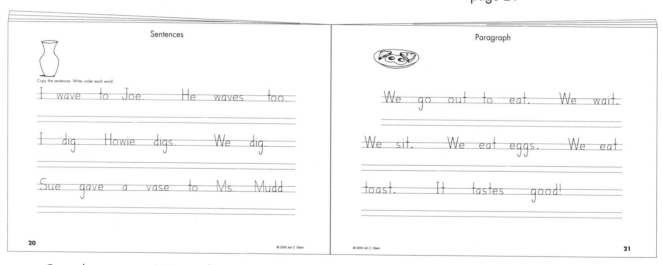

Rhyming Words

Read the words out loud. Listen! They rhyme!

Copy directly under each word.

wide side   toe doe   last cast

save gave   age cage   ice twice

© 2000 Jan Z. Olsen

19

- Read the words out loud.
- Children learn about sounds as they say the words. Beginning sounds are different. Ending sounds are the same. They rhyme!
- Copy directly under each word.
- Practice common letter patterns with rhymes—it is twice the fun.

Sentence practice
page 20

Sentences

Copy the sentences. Write under each word.

I wave to Joe.   He waves too.

I dig. Howie digs.   We dig.

Sue gave a vase to Ms Mudd

20   © 2000 Jan Z. Olsen

- Copy the sentence. Write under each word.
- Generous spaces give room to write.
- Practicing "action words" makes fun sentences!
- Capitalize the first word in a sentence, titles, and names (see *Printing Power,* page 48).

Paragraphs and exclamation points
page 21

Paragraph

We go out to eat.   We wait.

We sit.   We eat eggs.   We eat

toast.   It tastes good!

© 2000 Jan Z. Olsen   21

- Copy below the model.
- Paragraphs are a group of sentences about a subject.
- Teach the children about sentences and paragraphs. The sentences on page 20 are about three unrelated subjects. The sentences on page 21 are about one subject (breakfast) and make up a paragraph.
- The paragraph is indented. Explain this word and find indented paragraphs in books.
- Use the exclamation point to indicate strong feelings.

Teaching l

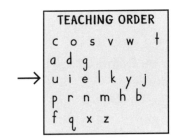

TEACHING ORDER

c o s v w t
a d g
→ u i e l k y j
p r n m h b
f q x z

Key Points: Letter l starts above the lines. It is as tall as L. It is easy to write.

Grade 1 - *My Printing Book*
page 30

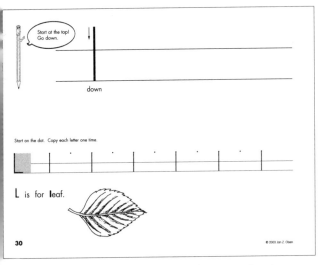

Extra: Read "L is for leaf." Move finger under the sentence from left to right. Students may color the leaf or draw pictures of things that begin with l (lemon, lion, lamp).

Grade 2 - *Printing Power*
page 22

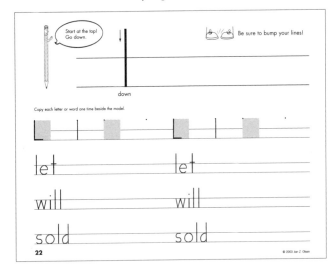

Lesson Plan

Demonstrate l
Show children how to make l on the board and/or in the workbook. Say the step-by-step directions as you demonstrate.

Teach in workbook
1. Read the directions.
   Finger trace the step-by-step models.
2. Find L on the gray block and l on the double lines.
   Copy the letters. Teacher should demonstrate, coach, and watch students.
3. Copy the word lists. Grade 1 teachers may assign one list now, another later.

Tip
- Teach that L and l are different, but both begin high above the lines.

Evaluate
- If l is too short:
  Tell students to begin l high above the lines.

Teaching k

Key Point: Letter k is as tall as K, but the "kick" is lower.

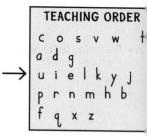

TEACHING ORDER
c o s v w t
a d g
→ u i e l k y j
p r n m h b
f q x z

Grade 1 - *My Printing Book*
page 32

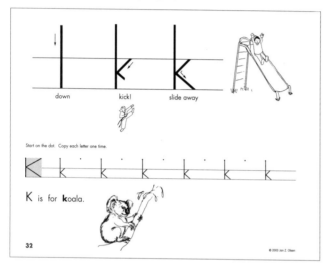

Extra: Read "K is for koala." Move finger under the sentence from left to right. Students may color the koala or draw pictures of things that begin with k (kitten, kite, king).

Grade 2 - *Printing Power*
page 23

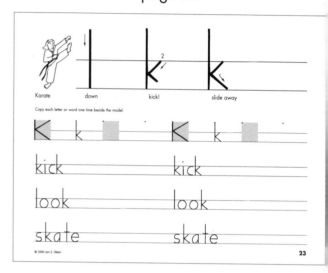

Lesson Plan

Demonstrate k

Show children how to make k on the board and/or in the workbook. Say the step-by-step directions as you demonstrate.

Teach in workbook

1. Read the directions.
   Finger trace the step-by-step models.
2. Find K on the gray block and k on the double lines.
   Copy the letters. Teacher should demonstrate, coach, and watch students.
3. Copy the word lists. Grade 1 teachers may assign one list now, another later.

Tip

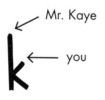

- Teach that the kick in k is lower. Use this story. "The big line is Mr. Kaye, your karate teacher. He wants you to demonstrate a kick. Put the pencil on the line. That's you. Now kick Mr. Kaye. That's the karate k."

Evaluate

- If the child confuses K and k:
  Explain that both are tall, but the kick for lowercase k is lower.

48

Teaching y

TEACHING ORDER

c o s v w t
a d g
u i e l k y j
p r n m h b
f q x z

Key Points: Letter y descends below the line. Lowercase y is like its capital, but it is placed lower.

Grade 1 - *My Printing Book*
page 34

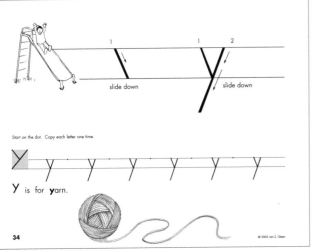

Extra: Read "Y is for yarn." Move finger under the sentence from left to right. Students may color the yarn yellow.

Grade 2 - *Printing Power*
page 24

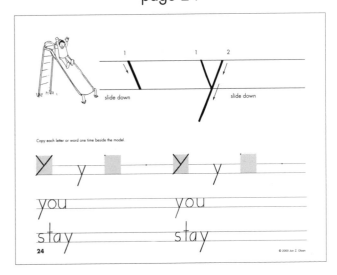

Lesson Plan

Demonstrate y

Show children how to make y on the board and/or in the workbook. Say the step-by-step directions as you demonstrate.

Teach in workbook

1. Read the directions.
   Finger trace the step-by-step models.
2. Find Y on the gray block and y on the double lines.
   Copy the letters. Teacher should demonstrate, coach, and watch students.
3. Copy the word lists. Grade 1 teachers may assign one list now, another later.

Tips

- Teach that Y and y are the same. They're just in different positions.
- Teach that y goes below the line.
- You or your student may choose another style for capital Y – Y.

Evaluate

- If student slides the stroke the wrong way:
  Count very slowly. One............Two................Which comes first? One.
  Make one slide down first. Slide the way the boy in the picture is sliding.

✓ **Check your teaching with** _I like you._
Ask child to print the sentence. Spell the words and watch. Did the child begin with a capital? Use space between words? Form and place letters correctly? End with a period? Reteach as needed. See page 68 of this guide for two sentence spacing activities.

Teaching j

Key Point: The lowercase j is similar to its capital, but has a different top and is placed lower.

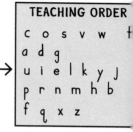

TEACHING ORDER

c o s v w t
a d g
u i e l k y j
p r n m h b
f q x z

Grade 1 – *My Printing Book*
page 36

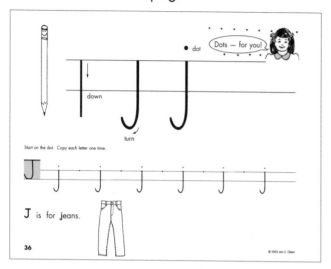

Extra: Read "J is for jeans." Move finger under the sentence from left to right. Students may color the jeans or draw pictures of things that begin with j (jellyfish, juice, jewel).

Grade 2 – *Printing Power*
page 25

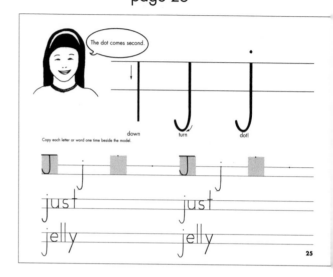

Lesson Plan

Demonstrate j

Show children how to make j on the board and/or in the workbook. Say the step-by-step directions as you demonstrate.

Teach in workbook

1. Read the directions.
   Finger trace the step-by-step models.
2. Find J on the gray block and j on the double lines.
   Copy the letters. Teacher should demonstrate, coach, and watch students.
3. Copy the word lists. Grade 1 teachers may assign one list now, another later.

Tips

• Teach that J and j are similar. Point out the differences. They start in different places. They have different tops.
• Teach that j goes below the line.
• J and j turn the same direction as lowercase g.

Evaluate

• If J or j curves too much:
   Make a "ruler" straight line down. Turn only at the bottom.

50

Grade 1 Practice

My Printing Book

Letter review
page 38

Sentence practice
page 39

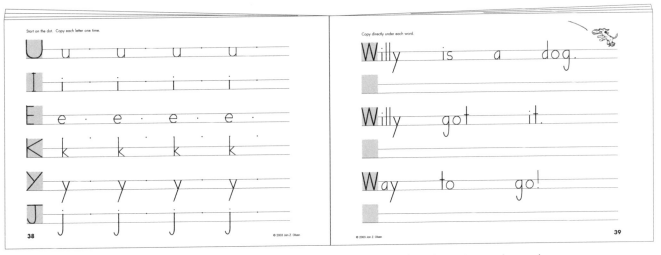

- Start on the dot.
- Copy each letter one time.
- Complete one column a day.
- Don't forget to bump the lines!

- Copy directly under each word.
- Don't forget the "nothing" after each word for good spacing.
- Introduce the exclamation point, to show excitement.

Second grade teachers, turn the page for your Grade 2 Practice!

2003 Jan Z. Olsen

Grade 2 Practice

Printing Power

Letter review
page 26

Singular and plural
page 27

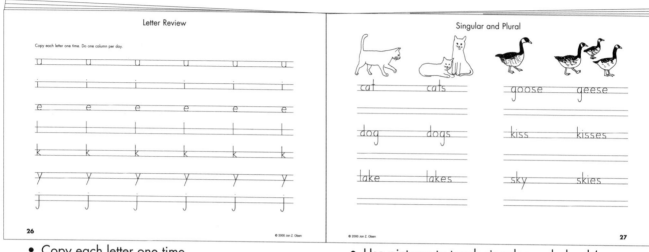

- Copy each letter one time.
- Focus on correct letter placement—fit u i e between the lines, l and k begin above, and y and j go below.

- Use pictures to teach singular and plural (one or more than one).
- Some plurals are easy—just add s.
- Other plurals are tricky.
- Practice making singular words plural.

Sentence practice
page 28

Paragraph practice
page 29

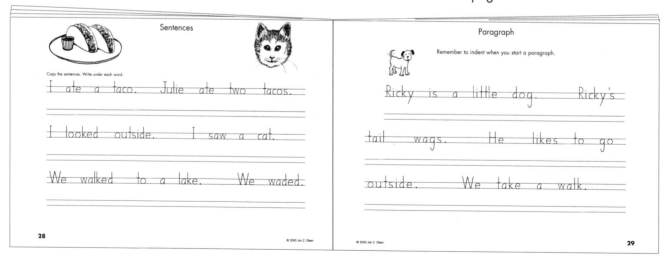

- Copy the sentences. Write under each word.
- Remember: Capital letters begin above the lines.
- Don't forget to bump the lines.
- Encourage children to draw or color on the page.

- Notice that the paragraph is indented for the student.
- A period comes at the end of each sentence.
- Compare page 28 (unrelated sentences) and page 29 (indented paragraph about Ricky).

Teaching the Diver Letters

THE DIVER LETTERS

p   r   n   m   h   b

Let's pretend we're divers! Stand up. Get ready!

Which way do you dive? **Down!**

Then what happens? **You come up!**

Then what do you do? **You swim over** ... on the top line!

When you come up, be sure to swim over **on the top line**.

30

© 2000 Jan Z. Olsen

Demonstrate basic stroke patterns

The diver letters, p r n m h b, all begin with this sequence:
1. Dive down.
2. Come up.
3. Swim over to the right.

To teach this group, follow the illustration. Have your class stand up, go through the steps of diving down, coming up, and swimming over to the side.

Demonstrate each letter with your finger

Face your class and draw a huge p in the air, saying "dive down, come up, swim over, and around." Have your students point to your index finger, following your motions. Repeat this demonstration with the other diver letters. Kids get a kick out of imaginary erasing between letters.

Important tip

When facing your class you must make the letters swim over to your left so they'll be right for your children. See above illustration.

Teaching p

Key Points: Letters p r n m h b are "diver" letters. They start with the same basic stroke pattern: dive down, come up, swim over.

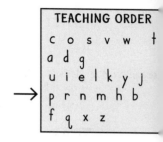

TEACHING ORDER

c o s v w t
a d g
u i e l k y j
→ p r n m h b
f q x z

Grade 1 – *My Printing Book*
page 40

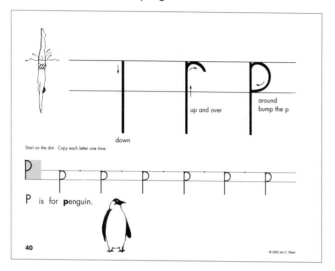

Extra: Read "P is for penguin." Move finger under the sentence from left to right. Students may color or draw pictures of things that begin with p (pail, popcorn, pants).

Grade 2 – *Printing Power*
page 31

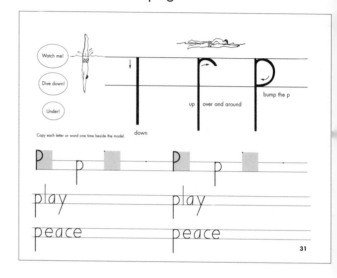

Lesson Plan

Demonstrate p

Show children how to make p on the board and/or in the workbook. Say the step-by-step directions as you demonstrate.

Teach in workbook

1. Read the directions.
   Finger trace the step-by-step models.
2. Find P on the gray block and p on the double lines.
   Copy the letters. Teacher should demonstrate, coach, and watch students.
3. Copy the word lists. Grade 1 teachers may assign one list now, another later.

Tips

- Teach that P and p are in different positions.
- Teach that p goes down below the line.
- Capital P has been taught with two strokes. Your students may make P with a continuous stroke.
- Have students stand and repeat diver motions, "Diver letters dive down, come up, and swim over." Write p in the air for them to finger trace with you.
- P is for purple too! Children may like to trace over the p with a purple crayon.

Evaluate

- If retracing is a problem:
  Say they are in a diving competition. They must dive down and come straight up in the bubbles.

54

Teaching r

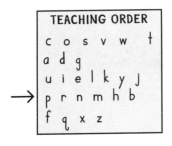

TEACHING ORDER

c o s v w t
a d g
u i e l k y j
→ p r n m h b
f q x z

ey Points: Letter r is for retracing! Teach your children to retrace (come up on the line) carefully. Letter r is the 10th most frequently used letter. It is also the basis for n and m. Teach it well!

Grade 1 - *My Printing Book*
page 42

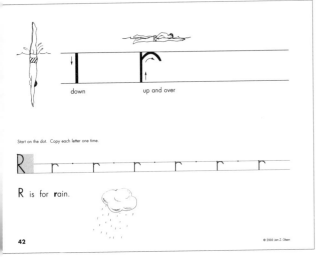

Grade 2 - *Printing Power*
page 32

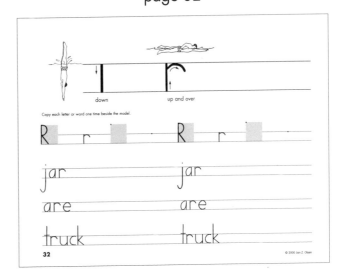

xtra: Read "R is for rain." Move finger under the entence from left to right. Students may color the rain or raw pictures of things that begin with r (ring, rose, rug).

Lesson Plan

Demonstrate r
Show children how to make r on the board and/or in the workbook.
Say the step-by-step directions as you demonstrate.

Teach in workbook
1. Read the directions.
   Finger trace the step-by-step models.
2. Find R on the gray block and r on the double lines.
   Copy the letters. Teacher should demonstrate, coach, and watch students.
3. Copy the word lists. Grade 1 teachers may assign one list now, another later.

Tips
- Teach that R and r are different.
- Have students stand and repeat diver motions, "Diver letters dive down, come up, and swim over." Write r in the air for them to finger trace with you.
- Letter r is for red. Students may trace over the r with a red crayon.

Evaluate
- If r isn't retraced:
  Say the pencil must retrace until it gets to the top line and can swim over.

Teaching n

Key Points: Letter n is the fifth most frequently used letter. Learning to make r prepared children for making n.

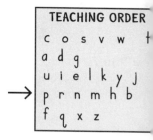

TEACHING ORDER

c o s v w t
a d g
u i e l k y j
→ p r n m h b
f q x z

Grade 1 – *My Printing Book*
page 44

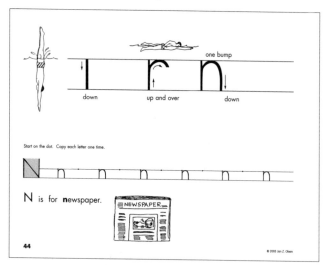

Extra: Read "N is for newspaper." Move finger under the sentence from left to right. Students may draw pictures of things that begin with n (nest, nose, net).

Grade 2 – *Printing Power*
page 33

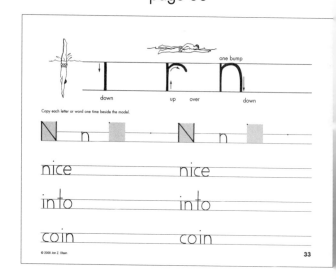

Lesson Plan

Demonstrate n

Show children how to make n on the board and/or in the workbook. Say the step-by-step directions as you demonstrate.

Teach in workbook

1. Read the directions.
   Finger trace the step-by-step models.
2. Find N on the gray block and n on the double lines.
   Copy the letters. Teacher should demonstrate, coach, and watch students.
3. Copy the word lists. Grade 1 teachers may assign one list now, another later.

Tips

- Teach that N and n are different.
- Have students stand and repeat diver motions, "Diver letters dive down, come up, and swim over." Then write n in the air for them to finger trace with you.
- This would be a good time to review the Frog Jump Capitals, especially P R N M B.

Evaluate

- If n isn't retraced:
  The pencil must retrace until it gets to the top line and can swim over.
- If n finishes with a slide:
  Teach that n comes straight down. No sliding allowed.

Grade 1 Practice

My Printing Book

Sentence practice
page 46

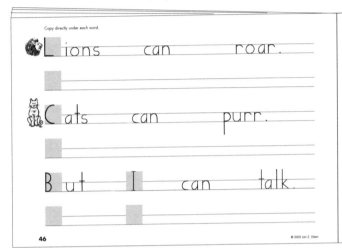

Sentence practice
page 47

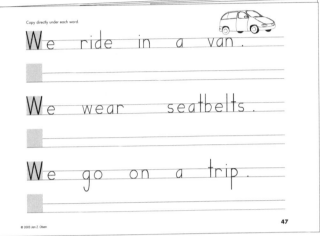

- Be sure children put letters in words close together.
- Teach that pronoun I is always capitalized.
- Have children make animal sounds.
- Make up other easy sentences with animals and sounds.

- Be sure children copy directly under the models.
- Help children place letters on line.
- Talk with children about transportation.
- Talk about things used to make activities safer—helmets, pads, seatbelts.

Teaching m

Key Points: Teach careful retracing. Learning n prepares children for making m.

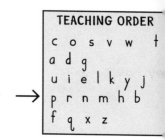

Grade 1 – *My Printing Book*
page 48

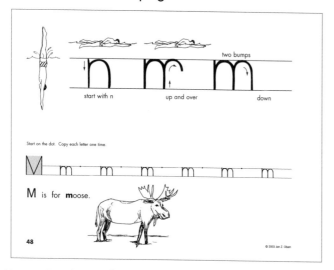

Extra: Read "M is for moose." Move finger under the sentence from left to right. Students may color the moose or draw pictures of things that begin with m (mouse, man, milk).

Grade 2 – *Printing Power*
page 34

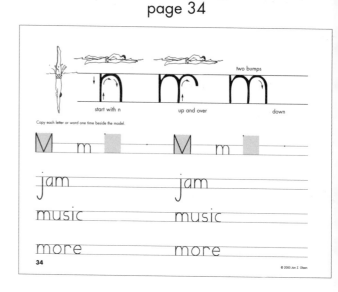

Lesson Plan

Demonstrate m

Show children how to make m on the board and/or in the workbook. Say the step-by-step directions as you demonstrate.

Teach in workbook

1. Read the directions.
   Finger trace the step-by-step models.
2. Find M on the gray block and m on the double lines.
   Copy the letters. Teacher should demonstrate, coach, and watch students.
3. Copy the word lists. Grade 1 teachers may assign one list now, another later.

Tips

- Watch to be sure students begin m on the top line.

Evaluate

- If m has gaps, refer to a trash can! If people throw trash in those gaps it would become a stinky m. Tell the students, "These gaps collect trash. That's a stinky m." Close the gaps to keep the bumps together. Leave just enough room for a chocolate kiss.

58

Teaching h

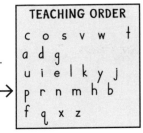

TEACHING ORDER

c o s v w t
a d g
u i e l k y j
→ p r n m h b
f q x z

ey Points: Letter h is the seventh most frequently used letter! Letter h begins high above the lines. Teach it as a high diver letter.

Grade 1 – *My Printing Book*
page 50

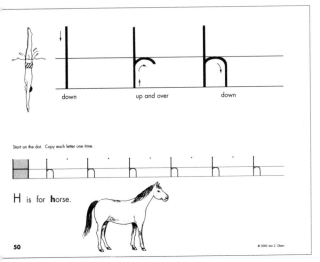

down   up and over   down

Start on the dot. Copy each letter one time.

H is for **h**orse.

50   © 2003 Jan Z. Olsen

Grade 2 – *Printing Power*
page 35

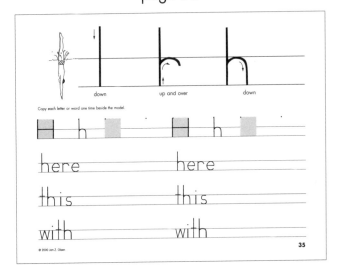

down   up and over   down

Copy each letter or word one time beside the model.

here   here

this   this

with   with

© 2000 Jan Z. Olsen   35

xtra: Read "H is for horse." Move finger under the ntence from left to right. Students may color the horse or aw pictures of things that begin with h (hat, hair, hose).

Lesson Plan

Demonstrate h
Show children how to make h on the board and/or in the workbook.
Say the step-by-step directions as you demonstrate.

Teach in workbook
1. Read the directions.
   Finger trace the step-by-step models.
2. Find H on the gray block and h on the double lines.
   Copy the letters. Teacher should demonstrate, coach, and watch students.
3. Copy the word lists. Grade 1 teachers may assign one list now, another later.

Tips
- Teach that H and h are different, but they both start high.
- Have students stand and repeat diver motions, "Diver letters dive down, come up, and swim over." Then write h in the air for them to finger trace. Have them reach high in the air to start.

Evaluate
- If h is too short:
  Emphasize the h as a "high" dive that starts way up in the air.
- If retracing is a problem:
  The pencil must retrace until it gets to the top line and can "swim over."
- If h finishes with a slide:
  Teach that h comes straight down. No sliding allowed.

2003 Jan Z. Olsen   **59**

Teaching b

Key Points: Letter b is taught much later than d to avoid b-d confusion. Letter b begins like an h.

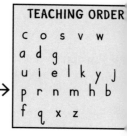

TEACHING ORDER
c o s v w
a d g
u i e l k y j
→ p r n m h b
f q x z

Grade 1 – *My Printing Book*
page 52

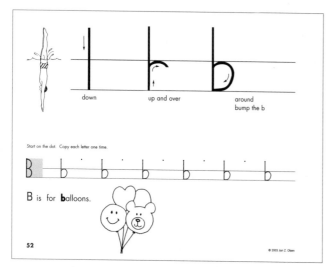

Extra: Read "B is for balloons." Move finger under the sentence from left to right. Students may color the balloons or draw pictures of things that begin with b (ball, boy, butterfly).

Grade 2 – *Printing Power*
page 36

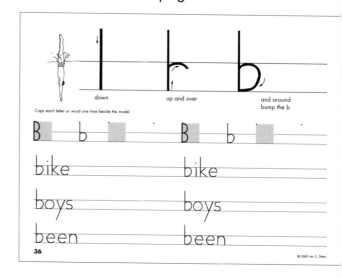

Lesson Plan

Demonstrate b
Show children how to make b on the board and/or in the workbook. Say the step-by-step directions as you demonstrate.

Teach in workbook
1. Read the directions.
   Finger trace the step-by-step models.
2. Find B on the gray block and b on the double lines.
   Copy the letters. Teacher should demonstrate, coach, and watch students.
3. Copy the word lists. Grade 1 teachers may assign one list now, another later.

Tips
- Teach that B and b are different.
- Have students stand and repeat diver motions, "Diver letters dive down, come up, and swim over."
- Write h in the air for them to finger trace. Say, "Here is an h for a honey bee." Turn the h into b.

Evaluate
- If reversals of b and d are a problem:
  Teach students to think of h for honey bee. This association will help.

✓ **Check your teaching with** __run   jump   bath__
Ask the child to print the words. Spell the words r-u-n, j-u-m-p, and b-a-t-h. Did the child use space between the words? Form and place letters correctly on the line? Use the diver motions for p r n m h b? Reteach as needed.

60

Grade 1 Practice

My Printing Book

Letter review
page 54

Sentence practice
page 55

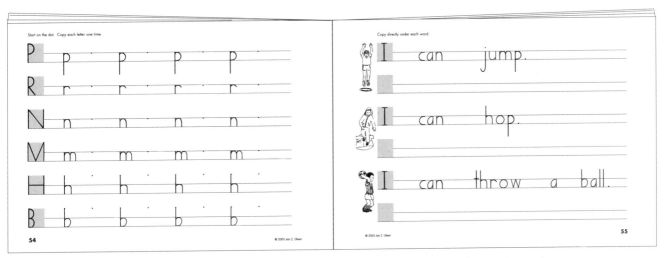

- Start on the dot.
- Remember to dive down, come up, and swim over.
- Don't forget to swim over on the top line!
- Complete one column a day.
- Have children do the motions of diver letters.

- Copy directly under each word.
- Gray blocks will help with capitals.
- The sample sentence formula "I can . . ." can lead to other sentences.
- What else can the children do?

Second grade teachers, turn the page for your Grade 2 Practice!

Grade 2 Practice
Printing Power

Diver letters review
page 37

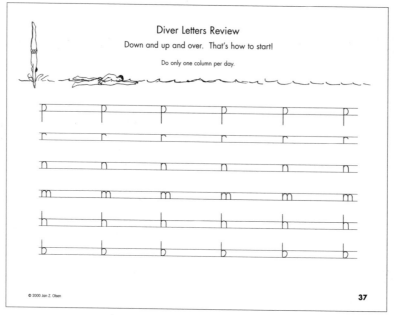

Diver Letters Review

Down and up and over. That's how to start!

Do only one column per day.

© 2000 Jan Z. Olsen

37

- Remember to dive down, come up, and swim over!
  Look at the model.
- Practice diver letters all week long.
- Have children do the motions of diver letters.

Sentence practice
page 38

Sentences

Copy the sentences. Write under each word.

John and Ruby sat on a bench.

The cat climbed up the tree.

Eric looked under his bed.

38

© 2000 Jan Z. Olsen

Paragraph practice
page 39

Paragraph

I have a stamp pad. I used

my thumb to make thumb prints.

Then I made them into animals.

© 2000 Jan Z. Olsen

39

- Copy the sentences.
- The sentences use prepositional phrases: on a bench, up the tree, under his bed. Make up other sentences.
- Remind children to begin copying under the first letter of each word.

- Paragraphs tell about one subject.
- Copy under each word.
- Can you make more animals with thumb prints?
- **Thumb prints** uses all six diver letters.

62

Teaching f

TEACHING ORDER					
c	o	s	v	w	t
a	d	g			
u	i	e	l	k	y	j
p	r	n	m	h	b
→ f	q	x	z		

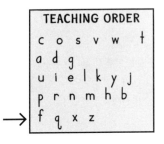

Key Points: Teachers, draw an arrow on the cross according to each child's handedness.
Right-handed children cross ⟶ . Left-handed children cross ⟵ .
Have students cross slightly above the guideline so that the pencil line shows.

Grade 1 – *My Printing Book*
page 56

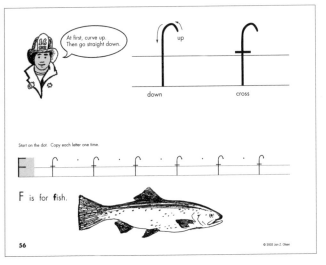

At first, curve up. Then go straight down.

up

down   cross

Start on the dot. Copy each letter one time.

F is for fish.

56   © 2003 Jan Z. Olsen

Grade 2 – *Printing Power*
page 40

At first, curve up. Then straight down.

up

down   cross

Copy each letter or word one time beside the model.

four   four
fish   fish
off   off

40   © 2000 Jan Z. Olsen

Extra: Read "F is for fish." Move finger under the sentence from left to right. Students may color the fish or draw pictures of things that begin with f (fan, feather, fork).

Lesson Plan

Demonstrate f

Show children how to make f on the board and/or in the workbook.
Say the step-by-step directions as you demonstrate.

Teach in workbook

1. Read the directions.
   Finger trace the step-by-step models.
2. Find F on the gray block and f on the double lines.
   Copy the letters. Teacher should demonstrate, coach, and watch students.
3. Copy the word lists. Grade 1 teachers may assign one list now, another later.

Tips

- Teach that F and f are different.
- Teach the stroke for f by talking about water squirting out of a fire hose. It goes up and then falls down. Most water fountains also squirt up and fall down in an f curve.

Evaluate

- Does f start correctly?
  Help students begin by going up, then turning and falling straight down.

Teaching q

Key Points: Letter q is a "Magic c" letter, but it is reserved until now to avoid confusion with g. Letter q is used very infrequently.

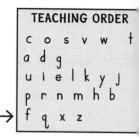
TEACHING ORDER
c o s v w   t
a d g
u i e l k y j
p r n m h b
→ f q x z

Grade 1 – *My Printing Book*
page 58

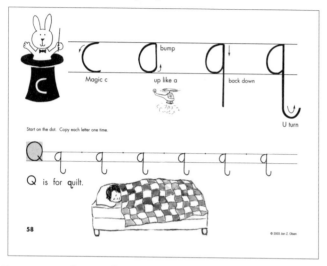

Extra: Read "Q is for quilt." Move finger under the sentence from left to right. Students may color the quilt or draw pictures of things that begin with q (queen, question mark, quill pen).

Grade 2 – *Printing Power*
page 41

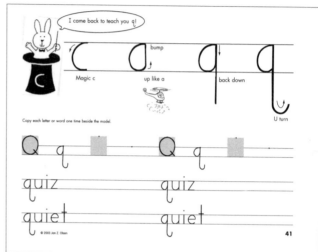

Lesson Plan

Demonstrate q

Show children how to make q on the board and/or in the workbook. Say the step-by-step directions as you demonstrate.

Teach in workbook

1. Read the directions.
   Finger trace the step-by-step models.
2. Find Q on the gray block and q on the double lines.
   Copy the letters. Teacher should demonstrate, coach, and watch students.
3. Copy the word lists. Grade 1 teachers may assign one list now, another later.

Tips

- Teach that Q and q are different.
- Teach that letter q is followed by u in words.

Evaluate

- If q is reversed:
  Student should pause at the end of the line and remember to make a u turn.

64

Teaching x

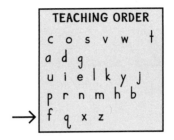
TEACHING ORDER

c o s v w t
a d g
u i e l k y j
p r n m h b
→ f q x z

Key Points: Letter x is very infrequently used. Your students know it from capital X.

Grade 1 - *My Printing Book*
page 60

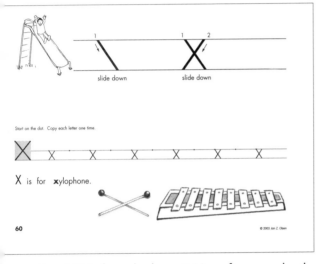

Extra: Read "X is for xylophone." Move finger under the sentence from left to right.

Grade 2 - *Printing Power*
page 42

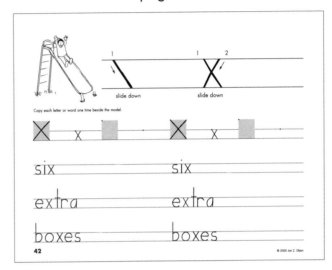

Lesson Plan

Demonstrate X
Show children how to make x on the board and/or in the workbook.
Say the step-by-step directions as you demonstrate.

Teach in workbook
1. Read the directions.
   Finger trace the step-by-step models.
2. Find X on the gray block and x on the double lines.
   Copy the letters. Teacher should demonstrate, coach, and watch students.
3. Copy the word lists. Grade 1 teachers may assign one list now, another later.

Tips
• Teach that X and x are the same, but x is lower.
• Show children how to play tic-tac-toe.

Evaluate
• If diagonal lines are a problem:
  Use the slate Wet–Dry–Try method described on page 18.
• If x is made incorrectly:
  Use the slate or gray blocks. X starts in the starting corner.
  The second line begins at the other top corner.

Teaching z

Key Points: Letter z is infrequently used. Your students know it from capital Z.

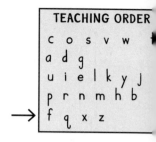

TEACHING ORDER
c o s v w
a d g
u i e l k y j
p r n m h b
→ f q x z

Grade 1 - *My Printing Book*
page 62

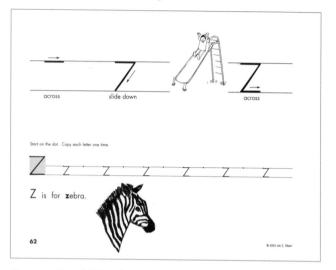

across   slide down   across

Start on the dot. Copy each letter one time.

Z is for **z**ebra.

62   © 2003 Jan Z. Olsen

Extra: Read "Z is for zebra." Move finger under the sentence from left to right. Students may make a zig-zag line.

Grade 2 - *Printing Power*
page 43

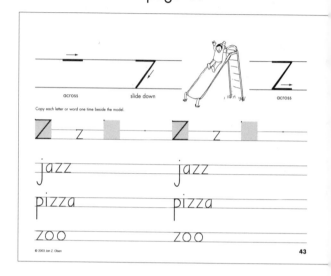

across   slide down   across

Copy each letter or word one time beside the model.

jazz   jazz
pizza   pizza
zoo   zoo

© 2003 Jan Z. Olsen   43

Lesson Plan

Demonstrate z
Show children how to make z on the board and/or in the workbook. Say the step-by-step directions as you demonstrate.

Teach in workbook
1. Read the directions.
   Finger trace the step-by-step models.
2. Find Z on the gray block and z on the double lines.
   Copy the letters. Teacher should demonstrate, coach, and watch students.
3. Copy the word lists. Grade 1 teachers may assign one list now, another later.

HANDWRITING WITHOUT TEARS®

Tip
• Teach that Z and z are the same, but z is lower.

Evaluate
• If z is reversed:
  Teach z on the slate. It starts in the starting corner.
  Use the Wet–Dry–Try method described on page 18.
  For right-handed children, they can pretend that the left hand is chasing the z at the beginning.

✓ **Check your teaching with** <u>fax   quiz</u>
Ask the child to print the words. Spell f-a-x and q-u-i-z. Did the child use space between words? Form and place letters correctly? Reteach as needed.

66   © 2003 Jan Z. Olsen

Grade 1 Practice

My Printing Book

Letter review
page 64

Sentence practice
page 65

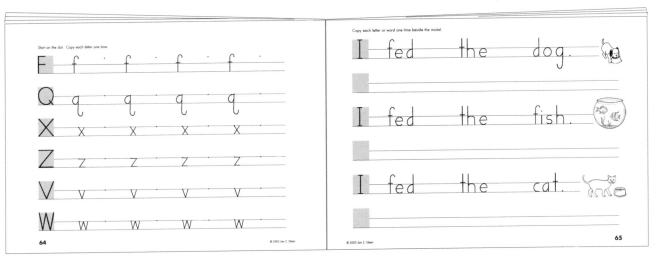

- Start on the dot. Copy each letter one time.
- Complete one column of letters a day.
- Don't forget to bump the lines!

- Copy directly under each word.
- What other animals can we feed?

Tomorrow's Lesson—Your Choice
- Use the Handwriting All Year activities on pages 80–84.
- Write new sentences and stories on the board.
- Demonstrate writing on our double line chart tablet.
- For solutions to specific handwriting problems, see the Help Index on page 85.

Second grade teachers, turn the page for your Grade 2 Practice!

Grade 2 Practice

Printing Power

Sentence practice
page 44

Sentence practice
page 45

• Review sentence skills, letter formation, capitals, and punctuation.

Sentence spacing
page 46

Sentence spacing
page 47

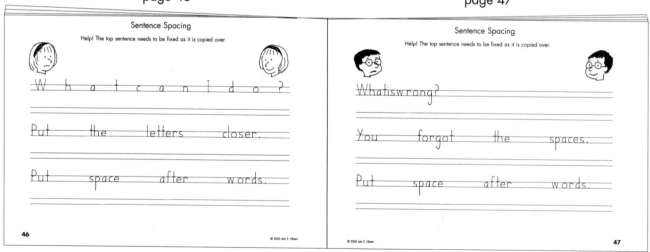

Help! Fix this sentence!
• The letters are too far apart.
• Circle each word in the top sentence.
• Now copy the sentence over, putting the letters closer.
• Copy the next two sentences.

Help! Fix this sentence!
• The words are too close.
• Underline each word in the top sentence.
• Now copy the sentence over with spaces between the words.
• Copy the next two sentences.

Grade 2 Practice

Printing Power

Capitalization
page 48

Capitalization

Complete these sentences. Practice capitals and periods.

Always use a capital to begin a sentence.

Capitalize the name of a person.

My   name   is

Capitalize days of the week.
(Sunday, Monday, Tuesday, Wednesday, Thursday, Friday, and Saturday)

Today   is

Capitalize months of the year.
(January, February, March, April, May, June, July, August, September, October, November, and December)

My   birthday   is

Capitalize titles (Mr., Ms., Mrs., and Dr.) and names.

My   teacher   is

Capitalize the names of towns or cities.

I   live   in

48   © 2003 Jan Z. Olsen

- Complete each sentence.
- Practice capitals and periods.
- Capital letters are used in special places.

Punctuation Marks
page 49

Punctuation Marks

Copy each punctuation mark.

Periods . _ _ _ _   Question marks ? ? ? ? ?   Exclamation points | | | |

Finish these sentences with the correct punctuation.

There are three kinds of sentences. Each kind uses a different punctuation mark at the end.

1. Put a period (.) after a sentence that states a fact.

    A sentence tells a complete thought___

    This sentence needs a period___

2. Put a question mark (?) after a sentence that asks a question.

    Do you know how to make a question mark___

    What day is it___

3. Put an exclamation point (!) after a sentence that shows strong feeling or surprise.

    This is an emergency___

    The house is on fire___

4. End these sentences with the correct punctuation marks:

    What time is it___   It is six o'clock___   Oh no, I missed the boat___

    Why are you crying___   I lost my dog___   Oh look, there he is___

    Cows have four legs___   How many legs does an octopus have___   Good for you___

© 2003 Jan Z. Olsen   49

- Punctuation is important!
- Use periods, question marks, and exclamation points!

More Capitalization Rules

Use a capital for:
- **Initials:** My initials are ___.
- **Holidays:** My favorite holiday is _____.
- **Languages:** I speak _____.
- **Names of mountains, lakes, oceans, and rivers:** The closest body of water is _____.
- **Names of schools or buildings:** My school is _____.
- **First word in quotations:** My friend said, " _____ "
- **First, last, and important words in titles:** My favorite book is _____.
- **Names of specific places:** I want to visit _____.
- **Pronoun** I.

Tongue Twisters
page 50

TONGUE TWISTERS

Copy each tongue twister. Then try to say . . .

slimy soap
blue bus
bed lamp
clean cat
cool school
go glow
so slow
flat frog

50   © 2003 Jan Z. Olsen

- Copy each tongue twister.
- Then try to say it three times.

Grade 2 Practice

Printing Power

The paragraphs presented on the next nine pages are about daily life or subjects that your students may study. The illustrations on each page give a clear sense of the subject. Based on this format, find other interesting pictures or objects to use as subjects for paragraphs.

Note to Grade 1 teachers:
These pages will give you ideas for teaching paragraph skills to your students. A picture or an object can be the subject for a paragraph. Write a paragraph on the board for your students to copy.

Paragraph practice
page 51

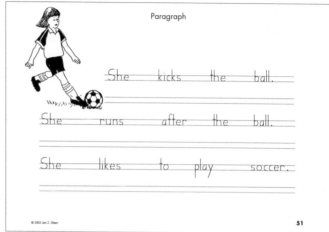

- Don't forget—indent!
- How will the paragraph end?
- Will she score a goal?

Paragraph practice
page 52

Paragraph practice
page 53

- Don't forget to leave space between words.
- Show your children a map of your region.

- Indent and copy under each word.
- Show the children a map of your state or province.

Grade 2 Practice

Printing Power

Paragraph practice
page 54

Paragraph practice
page 55

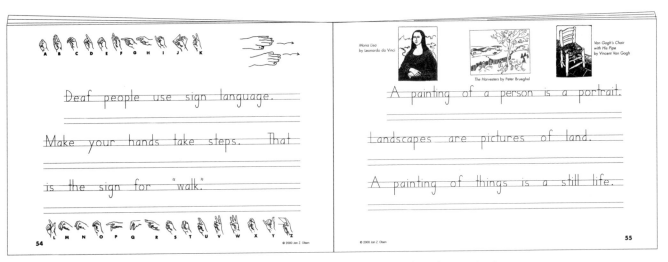

- Practice quotation marks.
- Children may learn to sign their names.

- Remember: bump the lines.
- Have children identify or draw portraits, landscapes, or still lifes.

Paragraph practice
page 56

Paragraph practice
page 57

- Review your comma rules.
- Practice number writing.
- 911 for emergencies.

- Practice exclamations.
- Do "Stop, Drop, and Roll" during recess.

Grade 2 Practice

Printing Power

Sentence practice
page 58

Paragraph practice
page 59

My dog is so smart. She
comes when I call. She can
sit and stay. She loves me.

58

© 2000 Jan Z. Olsen

The wing and tail feathers are
out. The claws are ready to grab.
The chickadee makes a landing.

© 2000 Jan Z. Olsen

59

- Discuss how some people need special equipment to help them in daily life.

- Review sequential order of sentences: what happened at the beginning, middle, and end?

Now turn to page 80 for additional activities.

72

Numbers Made Easy

Number Style

ur simple numbers are easy to write and reversal proof! Like the capitals, all numbers start exactly at the top.

1 2 3 4 5 6 7 8 9 10

Teaching Order

e teach the numbers in numerical order.
3 4 5 6 7 begin in the top left (starting) corner. This makes it easy for children to start them and it prevents reversals.
starts at the top, but in the center.
starts at the top, but in the right corner.
is made with 1 and 0. (Number 0 and Letter O are made the same way.)

Workbook Design

e teach numbers with the gray blocks, which are like pictures of the HWT slate chalkboard. The gray blocks prevent rever-
ls and help children learn to place the numbers.

2 3 4 5 6 7 8 9 10 O

ch number page also gives a review of previously learned numbers. The children practice writing num-
rs on gray blocks or on a single line. In second grade they also write numbers with no lines, like arithmetic papers.

+ | = ___ | + | = ___   2 + | = ___   3 + | = ___   4 + | = ___

Unique Teaching Strategy to End Reversals

achers know that marking reversals on math papers seldom does any good. Here is a strategy to use that will end even the
ost severe and chronic reversal problems. It will make you, the children, and the parents happy.
   1. Notice all the reversals on the math paper (perhaps 7 - 2 - 5)
   2. Correct only one reversal. Pick the lowest number (2)
   3. Help the child with that one reversal—the lowest number (2) only. Ignore the rest.

hat will happen?
   1. The child will be happy to see only one correction and will be receptive to help.
   2. The reversals will be gradually eliminated in an organized, orderly sequence.
   3. Every number will get as much help as it needs until the reversal is eliminated.

ow to help?
   1. Show the child the reversal.
   2. Use the appropriate teaching strategies to help him or her understand how to make the number correctly.

u will be delighted that you can organize your students. With the Wet–Dry–Try teaching strategy on the slate and/or the
ay block lessons, you can fix reversals. But don't stop as soon as they write numbers correctly. You have to over correct.
ay with it until the correct way becomes the automatic response.

Basic Lesson Plans: Use the plan below as a general guide for all numbers. Special tips for other numbers follow.

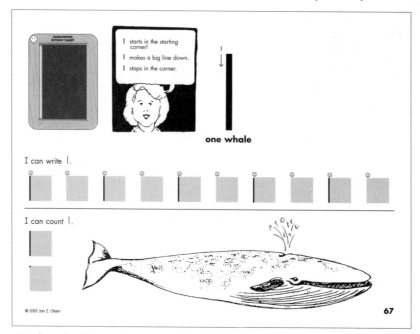

Numbers should be taught separately from handwriting, before a math-related activity.
HWT teaches numbers with the Wet–Dry–Try method on the slate and gray blocks.
Note: The number section in *Printing Power* starts on page 61.

Lesson Plan

Demonstrate |

Show children how to make **I** on the slate and/or in the workbook.
Say the step-by-step directions as you demonstrate.

Teach in workbook

1. Explain that the gray block is a little picture of the slate.
2. Find the starting corner. ☺
3. Copy the **I**. Teacher should demonstrate, coach, and watch students.
Note: Tell left-handed students to copy from the model on the right.

Tips

- Reading:
  Have students find and read the words "one whale." Talk about the word one and the symbol **I**. Students may also read "I can write **I**," "I can count **I**," and the directions.
- Coloring:
  Students may color the whale, and add water and sea animals. This is for children who finish first and like to color.

Evaluate

- Finger tracing the large number is a quick way to check the students' top-to-bottom habit before letting them practice.

TEACHING 2

ait until 1 is secure before teaching 2.
an the child write 1 correctly from memory?
se the basic lesson plan and these tips for 2.

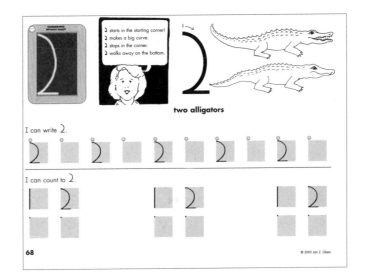

68

☺ Tips for 2

2 wants to start in the starting corner.

- Don't be anxious if 2 is a little fat, or a little skinny. As children gain skill, the 2 will develop a nice shape.
- Exaggerate pushing the chalk into the bottom corner of the slate (same with the pencil on the gray block). This promotes a nice sharp point.
- The little line ends just under the curve of the 2. Don't worry if it goes all the way across. This is not an important issue.

TEACHING 3

ait until 2 is secure before teaching 3.
an the child write 2 correctly from memory?
se the basic lesson plan and these tips for 3.

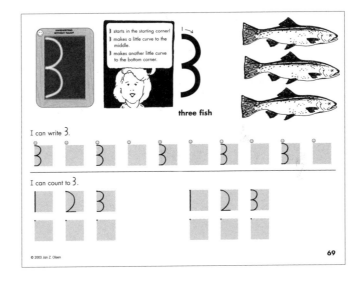

69

☺ Tips for 3

3 wants to start in the starting corner too!

- Some children have trouble finding the middle. Use a body image of a head (smiley face), tummy (middle), and feet (bottom of slate) to help them. It works for the gray block too.
- Make the chalk bump the wood at the middle. This promotes a nice sharp point.
- Don't worry if the little curves are fat, skinny, or not exactly equal. They'll improve.

TEACHING
4

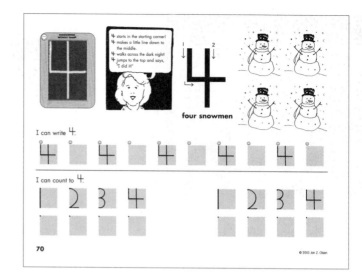

Wait until 3 is secure before teaching 4.
Can the child write 3 correctly from memory?
Use the basic lesson plan and these tips for 4.

☺ Tips for 4

4 wants to start in the starting corner too!

- Some children need help stopping at the middle. Ask the child to point to the middle before starting the little line down.
- Make sure the horizontal little line goes all the way across the slate or gray block.
- Add sound effects (ooo's) when 4 "walks across the dark night!"

TEACHING
5

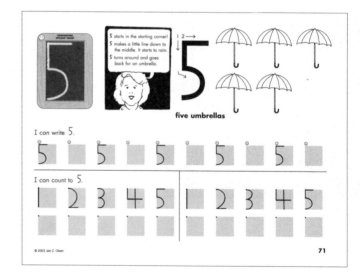

Wait until 4 is secure before teaching 5.
Can the child write 4 correctly from memory?
Use the basic lesson plan and these tips for 5.

☺ Tips for 5

5 wants to start in the starting corner too!

- Don't let children make 5 in a continuous stroke. That style deteriorates into an S shape with use.
- The two-step 5 stays neat in use.
- Expand the story by saying 5 is a bald man who walks down the street. He feels rain on his head, and turns around to go back for his umbrella. Tell them to look at the smiley face—that's the bald man.

TEACHING

six bears

I can write 6.

I can count to 6.

1 2 3 4 5 6

72

© 2001 Jan Z. Olsen

ait until 5 is secure before teaching 6. Can the child
rite 5 correctly from memory?
e the basic lesson plan and these tips for 6.

☺ Tips for 6

6 wants to start in the starting corner too! (Some people think it should start in the center, but if it did, it could be reversed.)

- Don't worry if it looks straight for awhile. With a little use, it will curve naturally.
- Don't worry about kids thinking it's letter b. (They don't use numbers and letters together until Algebra!)
- If you live in a hot climate, you can skip the bears. For example, in Texas 6 could be an armadillo.

TEACHING

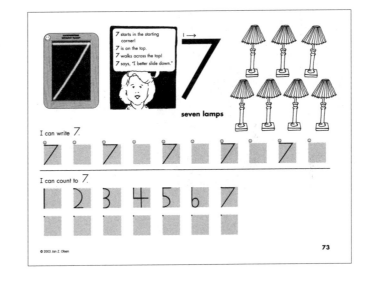

seven lamps

I can write 7.

I can count to 7.

1 2 3 4 5 6 7

© 2003 Jan Z. Olsen

73

ait until 6 is secure before teaching 7.
an the child write 6 correctly from memory?
e the basic lesson plan and these tips for 7.

☺ Tips for 7

7 wants to start in the starting corner too!

- Act out this 7 story for your students. Put a smiley face in the top left corner of a door frame. Reach up and put your fingers on the smiley face. Say that when you're out of the room 7 "walks" across the top of the door. "Walk" your fingers across the top. 7 hears you coming and says, "Get down fast! Here she comes."
- If you have a student who cannot do diagonals, the 7 can go straight down.

TEACHING 8

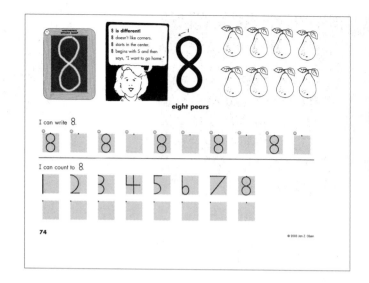

Wait until 7 is secure before teaching 8.
Can the child write 7 correctly from memory?
Teach letter S before 8.
Use the basic lesson plan and these tips for 8.

Tips for 8

8 starts in the center.

- 8 says, "I don't have any corners. I don't like corners. I won't start in a corner. I want to start in the center!"
- 8 (like I and O) is a symmetrical letter and can't be reversed.
- Starting 8 correctly can be a problem. Just pretend the 8 wants to go over to say "Hi" to the smiley face to start the first curve. Teach S before 8. If S has been learned, then 8 is easier.
- For both S and 8, children often stop after the first curve and don't know what to do. Tell them to "STOP, DROP, AND ROLL" (fire safety). This will get them going the right way. The repetitions of the Wet–Dry–Try activity are very useful for children who have trouble with 8.

TEACHING 9

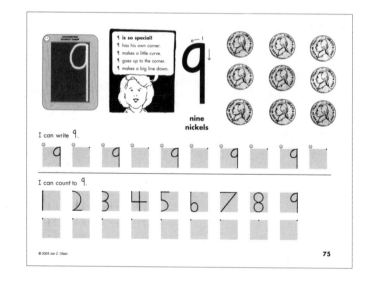

Wait until 8 is secure before teaching 9.
Can the child write 8 correctly from memory?
Use the basic lesson plan and these tips for 9.

Tips for 9

9 starts in the other corner (top right).

- Children get a kick out of 9 complaining about how long he had to wait for his turn. I say that 9 insists on having his own private corner.
- Use the helicopter image and sound effects.

TEACHING 10

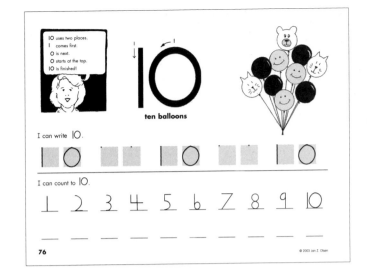

Wait until 9 is secure before teaching 10.
Can the child write 9 correctly from memory?
Use the lesson plan and these tips for 10.

Tips for 10

10 is the first time two places are used.
- Children already know how to make 1. It starts in the starting corner with a big line down.
- The zero begins at the top with a C stroke just like letter O.

Number Practice

Grade 1 - *My Printing Book*
page 77

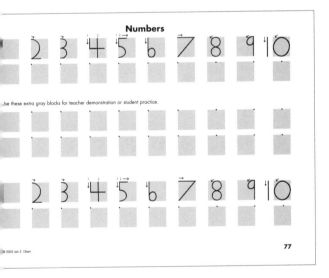

- Make copies of this page for extra practice.
- Student copies number below the model.
- Teacher may use the middle section to demonstrate.

Grade 2 - *Printing Power*
page 71

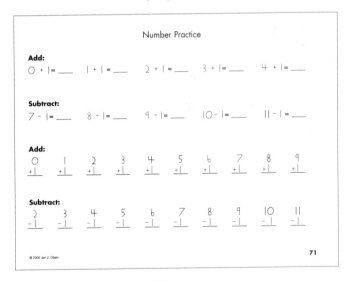

- These are easy problems.
- The purpose is to give practice using numbers in real arithmetic problems.
- Sometimes numbers are placed on a line.
- Sometimes there is no line.

Handwriting All Year

What now? Continue with short daily lessons to maintain and improve printing skills. Follow a weekly routine. On Monday a few capitals, Tuesday –a few lowercase letters, Wednesday – words, Thursday – sentences and Friday – fun and numbers.

MONDAY: CAPITAL LETTERS

Have a happy week! Start it by using one of these appealing activities.

1. CAPITAL REVIEW
(Prepare by copying page 6 from *My Printing Book* or *Printing Power*.)
- Take an alphabetical roll call. Call out A; if a student's name begins with A, everyone copies A. If not, leave it blank. At the end, the children can see all the capitals for their first names.
- Copy just the "Center Starters," A C G I J O Q S. Find them by looking at the dots at the top of the gray blocks. Color those blocks. Later, copy the remaining gray blocks, the "Starting Corner" letters.

2. A FEW RULES
(Prepare by enlarging and copying a paragraph from a book.)
- Children highlight all the capitals. Then talk about why each capital was used.
- Teach a few capitalization rules with this "About Me" activity.

About Me
Use cursive capitals.

My name is_____.
My initials are _____. _____. _____.
Today is _____.
My birthday is_____.
My favorite holiday is _____.
I speak _____.
I live in _____.
The closest body of water is _____.
My teacher's name is_____.
My school is _____.
My favorite book is_____.
My friend said, "_____."
I would like to visit_____.

Capital Rules
Use a capital letter for:

The first word of a sentence. People's names.
Initials.
Days.
Months.
Holidays.
Languages.
Cities and states.
Names of rivers, lakes, and oceans.
Titles (Ms., Mrs., Mr.) and names.
Names of schools or buildings.
First, last, and important words in book titles.
First word of a quotation.
The pronoun "I." Names of specific places.

3. REVIEW F E D P B R N M
(Prepare by copying page 3 from *My Printing Book* or *Printing Power*.)
Play the Mystery Letter Game to promote good habits for printing. This reinforces the habit of starting at the top. The game also corrects reversals. Use it frequently!

4. WRITE USA STATE ABBREVIATIONS (or just the beginning capital letter)
(Prepare by making copies of a USA map. This project will take a few Mondays.)
- Plan a trip and write the abbreviations for states you cross.
- Pick a letter and label all the states that start with that letter:

AL, AK, AR, AZ	KS, KY	RI
CA, CO, CT	LA	SC, SD
DE	ME, MD, MA, MI, MN, MO, MS,	TN, TX
FL	MT	UT
GA	NE, NC, ND, NH, NJ, NM, NV, NY	VA, VT
HI	OH, OK, OR	WA, WV, WI, WY
ID, IL, IN, IA	PA	

Tuesday: Lowercase Letters

On Tuesday, a few lowercase letters get all the attention!

Magic c Letters — c o a d g
(Prepare by copying *My Printing Book*, page 20 or *Printing Power*, page 14.)
* Show the children how you can make a Magic c Bunny out of a napkin. See page 36 of this guide for directions.
* Now play the Mystery Game for "Magic c" letters.

Diver letters — p r n m h b
Stand up! Lead the children in making the diver letter motions, down, up and over as shown on page 53. Now write the six diver letters in the air for your students to imitate.

Let's pretend we're divers!
Stand up. Get ready!

Which way do you dive?
Down!

Then what happens?
You come up!

Then what do you do?
You swim over ...
on the top line!

Same as Capitals — c o s v w x z
Teach a few capitals on the slate—C, O, S, V, W, X, or Z. Now write them as capital/lowercase pairs— C c, O o, S s, V v, W w, X x , or Z z.

Small Letters — a c i m n o r s u v w x z
(Prepare a page of double line paper with dots evenly spaced on the top lines. Children may be able to make the dots on double line paper with help.)
The children put their pencils on the first dot and wait for you to name a letter. Children must start the letter on the dot. Then go to the next dot and repeat. This will eliminate starting letters on the bottom line!

High frequency letters — e o a t n s
Re-teach one or more of these letters. Use the "Wet–Dry–Try" strategy (page 27).

Letter of the day with voices
Pick a letter, any letter! Re-teach the letter on the board using the "different voices" strategy (page 26). Children say the directions with you as you make the letter. Each time they use a different voice: regular- high – low - loud – soft – slow – fast.

Teach T and t.
Letter t is tall like T. Have students make capital T with their arms (page 34). Then make t by crossing the t lower. Tell students that both capital T and lowercase t are tall, but lowercase t is crossed lower.

'003 Jan Z. Olsen

Wednesday: Words

W is for words and Wednesday!
Focus on placing the letters next to each other correctly. Make lots of lists too!

1. Place words correctly on lines.

Write frequently used words to help with letter placement. Practice just one group and do them in order. Small letters give a home base from which to place other letters.
- Small letters – can, come, in, is, me, are, now, on, our, ran, soon
- Small and tall letters – and, red, at, eat, out, ask, cat, off , if, call, sack
- Small and descending letters – cap, nap, wig, say, my, many, carry, very

2. A preposition list!

(Prepare by gathering a toy and box. Use them to teach prepositions.)
- Invite a child to move the toy.
- Look at the toy's position. If the toy is inside the box, write "inside" on the board.
(Or write: outside, near, far, above, below, around, behind, beside, on, off, under)
- The children copy as you write. Repeat moving the toy and adding words to a list.

3. Rhyming words to practice diver letters — p r n m h b

If you reviewed these letters on Tuesday, make a list of words today. Choose from: man/pan, rub/tub, rib/bib, arm/ farm, run/fun, hen/pen, moon/noon, pen/hen

4. Rhyming words to practice Magic c letters — c o a d g

If you reviewed these letters on Tuesday, make a list of words today: Choose from: had/mad, dog/log, coat/goat, tag/bag, race/ face, age/page, dig/pig, rag/sag

5. Learn to write contractions.

Teacher demonstrates on board for students to copy. Turn two words into one short word. Put the words close together. Take out a letter and put in an apostrophe.

is not = isn't   I am = I'm
do not = don't   you are = you're
did not = didn't   he is = he's
was not = wasn't   she is = she's

6. Write the months. Begin with a capital letter.

Past   Last month was _____.
Present   This month is _____.
Future   Next month will be _____.

Write the word "ember." Now write Sept**ember**, Nov**ember**, Dec**ember**

7. Write common nouns and proper nouns in a list. Let children contribute.

boy = Patrick   girl = Meagan
dog = Clifford   mouse = Mickey
teacher = Mrs. Jones   puppet = Ernie

82

Thursday: Sentences and Punctuation

Thinking on Thursday! A sentence is a complete thought. Teach sentence skills today.

Sentence Spacing with Pennies
Give your children pennies or chips to use. Teach them how to look at a short simple sentence and fix the pennies to match as in this example.

 I  see a  dog.

Sentence Doctor
The teacher writes a "sick sentence" with the letters too far apart. The doctors fix it. They copy the sentence over and put the letters in words close together.

I a m h a p p y.   I   am   happy.

The teacher writes a "sick sentence" with no space between the words. Fix it!

Iliketowrite.   I   like   to   write.

Questions and Exclamations
Show students how to make a question mark. Write a question for them to copy. Show students how to write an exclamation mark. Write a sentence that shows strong emotion or surprise for them to copy.

Learn to Write Quotations
Bubble quotes make it easy to learn how to write quotations. Just follow this formula:
- Who (name)
- What (said, asked, shouted, yelled, cried, etc.)
    Now put a comma (,)
    Now put the first quotation marks (")
- Quote (Copy it exactly as it is written in the bubble.)
    Now put the last quotation marks (")

Use prepositional phrases
If you did prepositions on Wednesday, write one prepositional phrase today and use it in a sentence. See examples below:

He found his shoe **under the bed.**   The dog ran **around the house.**
The cat climbed **up the tree.**   He hid **behind the bush.**
She hit the ball **over the wall.**   The lion is **inside the fence.**

Friday: Fun And Numbers

1. End Number Reversals!
Use the "Wet-Dry- Try" strategy (*My Printing Book*, page 66 or *Printing Power*, page 60)

2. Correct arithmetic papers with the unique teaching strategy, page 73.

3. Names in the News
Make a list of three people who have their names on the front page of the paper. The next time you do this, add on to the list. Put a check beside repeated names.

4. Listen and Write Numbers
The teacher taps. Children count the taps and then write the number.

5. Today's Date
Review the correct number formation for all the numbers in today's date. Have student's write the date in this style:
_____-_____-_____

6. How old?
Write ages with words. For example: "I am seven years old."

7. Antonym (opposite) cards
(Prepare by writing some of these words on the board: big, near, hard, open, young, messy, heavy, dark, warm, ha fast, low, early, inside, up, in, curly, empty)
- Pass out cards
- Children copy one word (from the board) on the card
- On the back, they write the opposite word

8. Birthday Cards
(Prepare by passing out blank paper, crayons and stickers.)
- Show students how to fold paper to make a card.
- On the outside the students copy: Today is (date).
                                          Happy Birthday (Name !)
- On the inside write: From _____

9. Action! Act Out Verbs
(Prepare by writing some of these verbs (action words) across the board: sing, whistle, hum, smile, wink, laugh, cry, hop, walk, jog, run, clap, wave, shake, cough)
- You (or a student) act out one of the words. Underline the word.
- The children write a list of verbs as the acting continues.

HELP INDEX

Looking for help? This index and our website, www.hwtears.com, may have the suggestion you need. For additional help, ask for a consultation/evaluation by an occupational therapist.

Avoids printing
Decrease amount of writing. Select appropriate work for child's developmental level. Use appealing strategies such as "Wet–Dry–Try" lessons. See page 18 and 27. Give 5 minutes a day of individual help.

Capitals and lowercase letters mixed up
Check these separately. First ask child to write out just the capital letters on a single line as you dictate: "Capital A, capital B, etc." Check lowercase letters the same way, dictating "Lowercase a, lowercase b, etc." Teach as needed, being sure child know size difference for Cc Oo Ss Vv Ww Xx Zz and position difference for Pp. Use appropriate workbook pages for other letters.

Copying from board
If this is difficult, be sure it is not a vision issue. Otherwise, try moving the child's seat near the front of the room and be sure the child is facing the board. Using a slanted desk may ease the difficulty of moving the glance from a vertical to a horizontal surface. If the child is not ready for copying, let him watch you write and imitate you. Introduce near point copying at desk before far point copying from board.

Fluency
Not knowing letters well or forming them incorrectly causes fluency problems. Help the child master letters and use correct habits so printing will become automatic. The following pages of this teacher's guide are especially helpful: capitals—page 80, #3; lowercase letters—page 81, #1, 3, 4.

Left handedness
Handwriting Without Tears® is "left hand friendly." See pages 11–12 for paper placement and pencil position. See page 25 for practice and letter formation suggestions.

Line confusion
Simplify the lines and types of paper. Try to give size consistency. Use HWT double line wide or regular double lines. Determine optimal size by observing child's natural size while printing on just a single line.

Messy
The child may be rushing to finish or have too much work. Put the focus on doing less work but doing it well. Use HWT double line paper consistently. Show the child how to "bump" the lines. Bumping the lines helps children slow down to an appropriate speed.

Reading and phonics
You may modify the teaching order of individual letters as appropriate. Read page 22 for information about the HWT letter order. See page 16 for a delightful activity that teaches letter names and sounds.

Posture, paper or pencil concerns
See pages 9–13.

Reversals
For numbers, see page 73. For F E D P B R N, use page 19. Use page 40 for c a d g. Pages 61–62 review p r n m h b. Avoid b/d confusion by teaching d first and separately.

Memory
If child has to stop and think before starting to write a letter, this may be a memory issue. Try teaching just a few, high frequency letters (e o a t) until they can be remembered/written without effort. Then add letters gradually. See letter frequency list on page 22. Use the "Wet–Dry–Try" teaching strategy on page 27 to make letters more memorable.

Wordsruntogether
School papers may be the problem here. Frequently publishers do not give even a "finger" space between words. Exaggerate your spacing when you demonstrate. See page 24 and page 83,1 and 2.

Capitals, Numbers, and Lowercase Letters

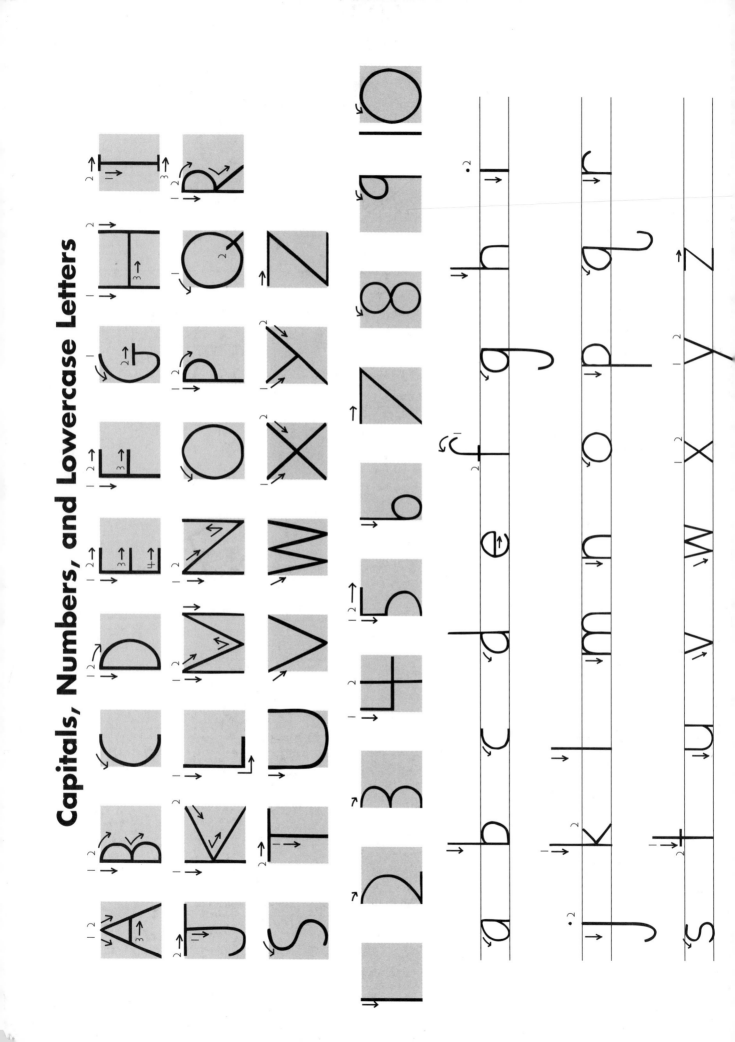